SALES NEW NORMAL
Re:think;
Sales Teams, Leaders, and Culture in the post-COVID era

세일즈 뉴노멀 SALES NEW NORMAL
by Hyosang Jang, Seungki Min
Copyright @ 2021 by Hyosang Jang, Seungki Min
All rights reserved.

First published in Korea in 2021 by Plan B Design
Translation copyright © 2022 by Hyosang Jang, Seungki Min
This English translation edition is published by POPPYPUB LLC arrangement
with Hyosang Jang and Seungki Min.
All rights reserved.

No part of this publication may be reproduced, stored or transmitted in any
form or by any means, electronic, mechanical, photocopying, recording,
scanning, or otherwise without written permission from the publisher.
It is illegal to copy this book, post it to a website, or distribute it
by any other means without permission.

Translated by Hyosang Jang, Seungki Min
Design by Lee Dahui

Published by POPPYPUB, Fort Lee
www.poppypub.com
poppypub is a trademark of POPPYPUB LLC.

Library of Congress Control Number: 2023934731

ISBN 978-1-952787-26-3 (paperback)
ISBN 978-1-952787-27-0 (ebook)

SALES NEW NORMAL

Hyosang Jang, Seungki Min

Re:think;

Sales Teams, Leaders, and Culture in the post-COVID era

PROLOGUE

I was talking to an acquaintance not long ago and heard an interesting episode. The acquaintance's little nephew was looking at a goldfish in a fish tank and tried to click on it and move it around. Why did this kid do that? Children these days have been growing up using devices such as smartphones and tablets since they were born, so from a child's point of view, clicking and dragging a goldfish in a fish tank is not an awkward behavior. The child's natural experiences have played a decisive role in creating his worldview. The worldview is the way or framework of looking at and interpreting the world. The worldview of the generation who used beepers or 2G phones and those who were naturally familiar with smartphones and tablets are bound to be different.

In human history, the emergence of automobiles has had a decisive influence on humanity's worldview. Before the advent of cars, wagons were humankind's most efficient means of land transportation. However, a wagon could only carry eight days' worth of hay, excluding shipment, so considering the return distance, it could only travel within four days. There was a length limit.[1]

With its many restrictions, automobiles quickly replaced the carriage after World War I. What is important is that these changes shift the worldview. The worldview of those who have ridden a carriage and those who have ridden a car is bound to be different. The hay that needs to be prepared for the carriage is not a factor to consider for automobiles (although we must think about fuel instead), and the distance traveled has increased dramatically, completely changing a person's worldview.

It is said that a person who lived in the worldview of carriage placed his world within a radius of 30km. Suppose you think about having this worldview for life. In that case, it isn't easy to meet new people other than your family members or neighbors or to have fresh thoughts or experiences, and you can only find your life partner within a narrow range. However, in the worldview of automobiles, the scope has expanded to more than 300km. Cars not only increased human behavior's radius but also significantly changed the real economy. First, with the popularization of automobiles and the development of road networks, residential areas expanded from downtown to out of town, which increased the value of suburban real estate. As the logistics distance increased, the logistics and distribution industries could develop together. All of these are difficult to think of through the worldview of wagons.[2]

A decisive event that shakes our worldview as much as automobiles are the epidemic. This is particularly the case with the pandemic, which brings tremendous changes worldwide.

> **Pandemic** According to the World Health Organization's guide, it is a world-class epidemic. It refers to the highest level of infectious diseases among the six stages of the epidemic influenza preparation guide.

Global infectious diseases are one of the least likely to occur for hundreds of years, including the Black Death, which killed one-third of Europe's population in the 14th century, the Spanish flu, which killed 50 million people on the European continent in 1918, and the Hong Kong flu, which killed 1 million people in 1968. However, these infectious diseases considerably changed human life, especially during the Black Death, which had a tremendous impact on all areas of medieval Europe, including politics, culture, economy, society, and religion. At that time, about 25 million people, or a third of Europe's population in the Middle Ages, died, resulting in a labor shortage, destroying the balance between the labor supply and demand, and leading to an improvement in the status of serfs. This soon led to the birth of capitalism. Not only this. The Black Death served as an opportunity to turn 'church-centered ideology' into 'humanist ideology.' This is because many people's belief that 'God will save us from illness' had collapsed. Due to this influence, the Renaissance period, which focused on literature and science rather than theology, arrived. The epidemic has become a decisive event that has changed society, economy, and culture. This changed not only medieval Europe but also the history and worldview of humanity.[3]

COVID-19 is becoming an infectious disease that has affected humanity as much as the Black Death. In other words, an event that could change humanity's worldview in the 21st century has occurred. It can be said that our lives are divided into before and after COVID-19. The era of 'New Normal' has arrived.

> **New Normal** This means that phenomena and standards that previously seemed abnormal are gradually becoming prevalent standards.

COVID-19 has dramatically changed our daily lives. Right now, restrictions on entry and exit, such as communications and exchanges between countries, overseas business trips, travel, and the closure of workspaces, have become so familiar. In particular, offline-based travel, distribution, education, and indoor sports activities were hit hard, and online-based businesses grew steeply. Companies' work has also changed rapidly based on non-face-to-face, making telecommuting a natural routine for even large domestic companies, which were conservative. In addition, as the period of not being able to go outside has lengthened, the home has become the center of the economy where people can relax, enjoy leisure and culture, and perform working tasks beyond simple residential spaces. Like the Black Death, COVID-19 has become a trigger that has changed society, economy, and culture.

Satya Nadella, CEO of Microsoft, said, "We have achieved all digital transformation that should have taken two years within two months of the outbreak of COVID-19." The threat of survival from COVID-19 accelerated cloud transition, 59% of global companies expected usage to exceed their previous plans, and 61% of companies set up cloud transition plans. Regarding the digital transformation trend by sector due to COVID-19, fitness, education, and courts are representative. U.S. users using digital fitness services increased by 30-35%. Lectures on group meeting platforms are conducted in the digital platform. No wonder, due to COVID-19, the e-commerce industry realized a 10-year transformation in only eight weeks, telemedicine (remote clinical services) 10 times the size in only 15 days, and the video streaming industry completed an explosive growth in 5 months which were only able to achieve with seven years of efforts in the past, and the views for remote educational services reached 250 million times in only two weeks.[4]

The way sales department works, leadership and culture we want to discuss in this book are also changing to suit the New Normal era. We are entering a new generation of 'Sales New Normal.' How should our sales leaders, teams, and members change and develop their capabilities when sales are being made non-face-to-face rather than face-to-face, and exhibitions and conferences are also being made through digital platforms? This book was written to solve the abovementioned concerns and aimed at helping readers through various examples and cases we experienced after the outbreak of COVID-19. For readers who read this book, we hope this book will serve as an opportunity to point out the direction of change and analyze the points to be considered in the era of 'Sales New Normal,' as well as set up the tone for later success in the trend of change.

CONTENTS

PROLOGUE 2

Chapter 1
Sales New Normal #1
The changes brought by COVID-19

How should sales change during this strategic inflection point? 14
  Are you aware of change? 19
  A salesperson's response strategy in the Post-COVID era 21

Everyone's hard-pressed because of COVID-19? Stop hesitating, and try out the formula for success in the post COVID era 23
  CASE STUDY [PEPSICO] Diversification of distribution channels 24
  CASE STUDY [Audi, Hyundai Motor Company] Online sales through digital consulting 29
  CASE STUDY Digital pivoting: BTS, My Real Trip 34
  Now, it's time to change our perceptions 38

Chapter 2
Sales New Normal #2
Changes in the way you work

In the New Normal era, how should sales departments' work change? 42
  CASE STORY 1 Salespeople are in danger due to COVID-19 43
  Change 1: Switching from offline to digital 45
  Change 2: Increased importance of data and information distribution 50
  Change 3: Changes in the way salespeople work 57
  Change 4: The role and necessary competencies of the sales department 61
  [CHECKLIST] Post-COVID era, sales department diagnosis table 69

Chapter 3
Sales New Normal #3
Changes in performance management

In the New Normal era, what is the key to sales departments' performance management? 72

    CASE STORY 2 Errors in performance indicators and goals   73

With the changing environment due to COVID-19, should the sales departments be controlled and managed? 78

Which performance indicators are most suitable to the New Normal era? 81

    Solution #1. Abandon your blind belief in measurement indicators.   82
    Solution #2. Pivot performance indicators, based on how realistic they are.   85
    Solution #3. Change the evaluation and reward system.   88
    CASE STUDY [Adobe] Check-in method and process   89

Points of "performance management" sales leaders should think of in the New Normal era 93

    Should you control them? Or give them autonomy?   93
    Extrinsic motivation vs. Intrinsic motivation   97
    Top-down goal-setting vs. Bottom-up goal-setting   103
    Mechanical approach vs. pursuing diversity   106
    [CHECKLIST] Post-COVID era, sales leader's performance management diagnosis table   109

Chapter 4
Sales New Normal #4
Changes in fostering and coaching

What are the sales leaders' roles and necessary competencies in the New Normal era? 112

    CASE STORY 3 New Normal era, 'Leader's thoughts vs. Members' thoughts' 113

    Changes in the role of sales leaders: autocratic leadership no longer works 116

    Sales leaders' coaching method: change the theme and style 120

    Sales leaders' competence development: keep up with the times 122

In the New Normal era, sales coaching & non-face-to-face communication 126

    CASE STORY 4 'The telecommuting issue' in the post-COVID era 126

    Sales Leader's Coaching: escape from experience-based habitual thinking 131

    Non-face-to-face communication of sales leaders: communicate constantly with team members 137

'Fostering/coaching' points that sales leaders should think of in the New Normal era 146

    Open learning vs. Enclosed learning 150

    Approaches to maximize Productivity vs. Creativity 148

    Control the information vs. Share the information 151

    Growth mindset vs. Fixed mindset 156

    [CHECKLIST] Post-COVID era, sales leader's leadership/coaching and communication diagnosis table 160

Chapter 5
Sales New Normal #5
The operation of a sales department

In the New Normal era, what is the ideal way to operate a sales department? 162

    CASE STORY 5 A sales department's operations and transition of roles 163

    Solution #1: Sales department, be an insider 168

    Solution #2: Integrate the strategy and execution 176

    Solution #3: Reduce the gap and strengthen the power in strategy execution 182

    Solution #4: Make the role of sales essential in product development as well 184

    An organizational structurematrix organazation that enables the sales department to actively participate in the development and the changes in development method 188

    CASE STUDY [Spotify] Spotify's Matrix organizational structure 189

The 'Agile Management' that sales leaders should consider in the New Normal era 198

    The background and basic principles of Agile Management 198

    Traditional management vs. Agile management 202

    The misunderstanding of "horizontal leadership" 204

    Agile culture, and culture of the MZMillennials and Gen Z generation 207

    [CHECKLIST] Post-COVID era, organizational operations, and agile management diagnosis table 210

Chapter 6
Sales New Normal #6
Let's start for change

In the New Normal era, Requirements for change in the sales departments   212

  CASE STORY 6 A sales department's operations and transition   212
  Organizations resist change by nature   214
  "Silence is golden(?)" Team members who do not speak up   218
  A culture of sharing information and accepting failures   221
  Collective/group intelligence over groupthink   224
  A culture that only values results? No! A culture that takes process into account? Yes!   226
  Now, it's time to strengthen the resilience of the sales department   229
  Ultimately, it's a matter of perspective   232

EPILOGUE   234

REFERENCES   238

Chapter 1

Sales New Normal #1

The changes brought by COVID-19

How should sales change during this strategic inflection point?

🚩 This is the story of the Black Death, which struck Europe around 1347. The Black Death was not just a disease that killed countless people, but also an event that had a tremendous impact on world history. With the Black Death reducing Europe's population and ravaging its economy, Europeans turned overseas. As imperialism consequently spread, European countries began colonizing the Americas, Asia, and Africa, and discovering the new continent, Australia. The Black Death marked a milestone in world history.

> This disaster caused numerous casualties on the European continent. This terrible epidemic indiscriminately attacked men and women of all ages. The ratio of deaths to the total population was higher than that of natural disasters and plagues over the past 2,000 years. In five years, close to two-thirds of Europe's population died from the disease, and most of the bodies were burned or buried in pits at once to prevent the spread of the epidemic.[1]

In 2022, although we are not aware of it, we may be in the middle of a historical event that will tremendously impact human history. COVID-19 has killed 6.5 million people worldwide and 627 million confirmed cases (as of October, 2022). The reason these numbers are not even higher is due to the development of science, which allowed us to respond well to the disease. If COVID-19 had broken out in the past, it would have had a more significant effect than the Black Death.

Our lives have changed significantly after COVID-19. There have been many changes, not only in everyday life but also in the workplace. Instead of working in the office, working at home and sharing opinions through online video conferences—rather than gathering in the conference room—became a daily routine. Now that most of the work previously done offline is being done online, and we know that most offline tasks could be successfully replaced with online procedures, we will not be able to go back before COVID-19, even when the pandemic ends. In that sense, the post-COVID era will bring new changes and challenges. And the future results can vary significantly, depending on how you adapt to the changing environment.

In particular, this is a time when people who work in sales and marketing jobs, who used to meet customers and create various opportunities offline, are more concerned about how to respond to these changes. We are at a strategic inflection point regarding whether to change the way we have been working, in line with the new pattern of remote work, and how to navigate that change if so.

The expression, Strategic Inflection Point[SIP], first used by former Intel CEO Andrew Grove, refers to a specific time when fundamental changes occur in corporate survival and prosperity. Companies make difficult decisions during strategic inflection points, and relevant coping mechanisms are firmly adopted.[2]

Strategic Inflection Point

Performance management and sales (Business) have become more critical in the post-COVID-19 era
→ **In order to active sales activities**, it is time to think and make efforts to maximize efficiency and performance.

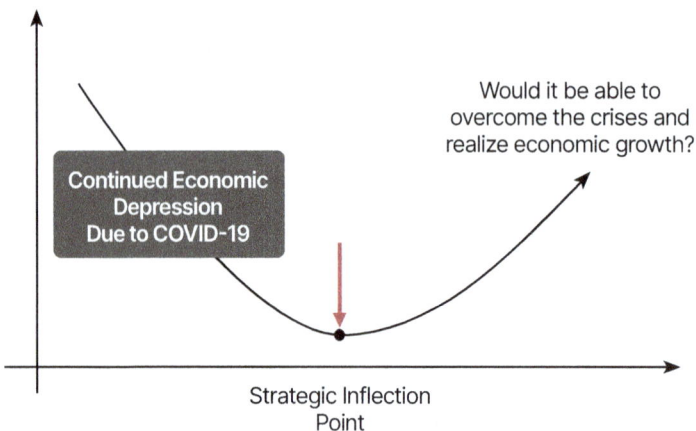

Depending on how you respond at the strategic inflection point, you will be able to survive the post-COVID-19 era and dream of a new leap forward. Then, what is the proper sales method to follow during this period of SIP? Let's take a look at some examples.

A, the owner of a self-employed business is busy, even during the COVID-19 era. How is A's restaurant doing well in this challenging time? A, who ran a high-end dining restaurant, also faced difficulties in the early days of COVID-19. The number of customers unavoidably plunged due to the second phase of social distancing, as sales of the dining restaurant, which was previously doing well in the evenings, plummeted since it needed to be closed after 9 p.m. At first, A could not find a way to overcome the difficulties.

Since this was a high-end dining restaurant, with all the fixed costs going into the regular operation, it was not easy to boost sales as much when customers were reluctant to eat out.

After much consideration, A's solution was to introduce a delivery system, like other restaurants. With the development of new menus, such as meals and wine suitable for delivery, and by introducing a delivery system, sales recovered a little. Since the delivery system was quickly introduced compared to other large dining restaurants, and thanks to the existing customers that ordered take-out, the restaurant held out to some extent. Still, it was difficult to recover their previous sales with the delivery service alone. A's worries deepened due to the continuous operational deficit. A went one step further from there, thinking that although delivering cooked food was good, it would bring more joy to the customers if they could cook the meal themselves. This was consistent with the restaurant's operational direction, and expected to make additional profits. In fact, in recent years, the HMR (Home Meal Replacement) market has been growing steadily, and some hotels have gained massive popularity by launching hotel food as meal kits. Since A continued monitoring and paying attention to these changes, he thought he could use this method and immediately implement it. As a result, it was possible to generate profit even in the COVID-19 era.

The above story is an adaptation of an actual case of a high-end dining restaurant in Korea. Although many industries are suffering from COVID-19, I wanted to show that recovery from the economic depression is possible, and has been successful in some cases.

Looking at the size of the market after the outbreak of COVID-19, the HMR market is expected to be around 4 trillion won, and meal kits, which can be enjoyed only with some simple cooking, are approximately 100 billion won (based on the Korean market in 2020).[3] In line with these changes in the market, A's strategy was fortunately successful. A took a step further, and produced various content such as real-time recipes and meal kit tips via live commerce and YouTube channels, to succeed in pivoting reliably. Pivoting in business is used to define start-ups changing their businesses by modifying products or strategies, a widely known concept by Eric Ries, author of The Lean Startup.[4]

A's experience can be considered a successful case of pivoting. A was among the first group of people who thought about the characteristics of the COVID-19 era, and applied them to their businesses.

A was aware of the needs of consumers who were tired of cooking—because they were spending longer time at home with their families, and cooking more and more—as well as those who were bored of take-outs or pre-cooked food. And based on these characteristics, the business direction was shifted to conducting online sales and delivery, and real-time, live cooking classes that were never tried before.

In fact, in the post-COVID era, we can find cases where people responded successfully by pivoting, such as drastically reducing offline stores and converting them into delivery stores to survive. The COVID era is indeed a challenging time for everyone. However, not all have failed to adapt. We then must consider what led these people to success, and benchmark their process.

Are you aware of change?

The bottom line is: are you responding positively and aware of the changes? In the previous case, if A had insisted on what he was familiar with, or failed to recognize the customer's needs and trends in a rapidly changing environment, he would still be experiencing various difficulties. His business may not have been able to survive the pandemic. The problem is that it is not easy to recognize the change. People often think they respond well to change, and are aware of it. However, we often fail to recognize its consequences around us, since we tend to only focus on what we are used to or interested in.

Let's look at the results of an experiment, to see how much people pay attention to change. A few years ago, National Geographic conducted an interesting experiment. The production team secretly installed cameras on a crowded street, and hired actors. First, actor A asked pedestrians for directions as follows.

"Excuse me. Where is the subway station? I've been looking for it but can't find it."

Then, two people carrying large boards would suddenly appear, and walk between the pedestrians and the actor. In the meantime, actor B, who looked completely different from actor A, would appear and replace actor A. Surprisingly, more than half of the people did not notice that the person they were talking to had changed from A to B.

The production team then conducted an even more interesting experiment. Would people be able to notice the change if the gender of the person they spoke to changed as well? They decided to find out, by replacing actor A, a man, with actor B, a woman. What was the result? People failed to notice even when the gender of the speaker changed.[5]

This phenomenon is called "Change Blindness" or "Inattentional Blindness." It refers to a situation in which changes occur but are not recognized.[6, 1)]

People are more insensitive to change than they think. Even though extreme changes such as COVID-19 have changed our lives, there are many cases where people still act the way they used to, or fail to recognize changes around us. The same applies to the business environment. Though changes have occurred in many aspects, including how people, customers, and industries work, many organizational members display "intentional blindness," by either refusing to acknowledge change because of the expectation that things will return to the previous state, or because their perception of change failed to keep up with the pace of change in reality.[7]

Intentional change blindness and inattentional blindness can be easily identified in the operational departments of businesses. This phenomenon is more pronounced among sales managers, because they still perceive offline and traditional relationship-oriented sales as essential activities. In this period of strategic inflection point, it is necessary to ask oneself, "Am I experiencing change blindness? If not, how should I respond to this strategic inflection point?"

Let's see some examples of how we should respond.

---

1) **Change Blindness and Inattentional Blindness:** Change blindness means not noticing apparent changes, and inattentional blindness means not noticing unexpected changes. Both refer to experiencing changes without being aware of them.

A salesperson's response strategy in the Post-COVID era

CASE 1 Salesperson A: "Nothing changes, so let's just wait."

Manager A, who works for an overseas sales team, has been so busy that he spent about three-quarters of a year abroad, managing exhibitions and marketing campaigns, until COVID-19 broke out. Like A, it was not easy for the team members of the overseas sales team to gather in one place, because they had to spend a long time in their designated area. Then, one day, COVID-19 changed everything in the world, and offline sales activities became impossible. At first, A expected things to return to normal in a couple of months, postponed exhibitions and offline activities, and waited for the situation to resolve itself. But nearly a year passed, and exhibitions and various conferences that had been delayed repeatedly were canceled, or took place online. The problem is the situation itself. It will take time for vaccines to spread worldwide and for everyone to be vaccinated, and even variant viruses have begun to appear. However, A waited with hope since vaccines were coming out. This is because there is a high risk of trying something new, and A's customers do not yet demand significant changes. A repeats, "At times like this, I should just lay low. If I try to do something, I'll have to bite the bullet…"

CASE 2 Salesperson B: "Let's respond to change with change!"

Assistant manager B, in charge of other regions in the same team as A, was visiting overseas workplaces and conducting investigations and analyses. However, COVID-19 spread, and inevitably, B had to stop the ongoing work. Though B was unfamiliar with the changes resulting from COVID-19, B found that there was no significant difference in terms of their work. This is because most sales with overseas agencies were conducted online. For essential exhibitions and conferences, it was necessary to visit and check the dealer or agency once or twice a year. Still, they adopted the non-face-to-face methodology, due to costs and efficiency.

As a result, B became very interested in using the PRM^(Partner Relationship Management) system, and had already launched SNS channels such as YouTube a few years ago, to promote products. Even now, when COVID-19 has encroached on the world, B insists that the changes will continue and is still struggling to find and introduce new ways or methodologies to respond to the changing environment.

In the above two cases, A does not acknowledge the change or respond proactively, while B accepts the change and responds positively. However, we cannot say that any of them is absolutely correct based on the above cases alone. If A was performing well with their existing business methodology, it might have been proper to focus on vital areas. However, it can be said that A is in a state of change blindness, and will respond bluntly to the upcoming changes. Salespeople must acknowledge the forthcoming changes and prepare more proactively for the post-COVID era, as these changes are deeply related to their survival. The post COVID-19 world did not just transform the type of work performed, but also made people question why sales should exist in the first place. In other words, it is necessary to recognize that even though this tragic situation may improve due to the emergence of COVID-19 vaccines or treatments, business activities ultimately cannot return to the past.

Everyone's hard-pressed because of COVID-19? Stop hesitating, and try out the formula for success in the post COVID era

In 2020, many companies suffered from COVID-19. Most countries' economic growth rate was stalled: the United Kingdom had a -11.2%, France a -9.1%, Germany a -5.5%, Japan a -5.3%, and the United States a -3.7%. Korea, as of December 2020, was also forecasting unprecedented reverse growth at -1.1%. Except for some companies that have online-based businesses, industries such as offline-based travel, distribution, performance business, and dining out have suffered unprecedented difficulties and are continuing to overcome the crisis.[8]

However, even in difficult situations where everyone is struggling, some companies or cases overcome these difficulties, continue to grow and succeed. So, what is the driving force behind these successes? In these case studies, we can find ways to overcome the period of the strategic inflection point in the COVID-19 era. I would like to introduce you to several eye-catching such cases.

20-year growth forecast for the top five OECD countries and major member countries

Rank	Country	Growth rate	Rank	Country	Growth rate
1	South Korea	- 1.1%	8	US	- 3.7%
2	Norway	- 1.2%	19	Japan	- 5.3%
3	Türkiye	- 1.3%	21	Germany	- 5.5%
4	Lithuania	- 2.0%	32	France	- 9.1%
5	Ireland	- 2.2%	36	England	- 11.2%

As of December 2020

CASE STUDY

[PEPSICO] Diversification of distribution channels

The world as a whole has been hit hard by COVID-19, but the United States is the country that has taken the hardest hit. The U.S. unemployment rate rose from 4.4% in March 2020 to 14.7% in April 2020, the most significant increase since statistics began to be compiled in 1948. Consumer psychology and purchasing behaviors were dampened significantly due to sluggish economic activities and shrinking job markets. The number of confirmed COVID-19 cases in the United States is increasing by around 40,000 a day, and it is unclear when things will return to normal. Retail sales in the U.S. also fell 14.7% in April 2020, the most significant decline in history. As the shutdown continued, the growth for most items except food and daily necessities fell.[9]

In this situation, most retailers are struggling, but it is worth paying attention to PEPSICO's response, the company behind Pepsi. According to PEPSICO's sales status, the company's growth slowed down slightly in the early days of COVID-19 but rebounded rapidly, exceeding the previous year's sales in August 2020.

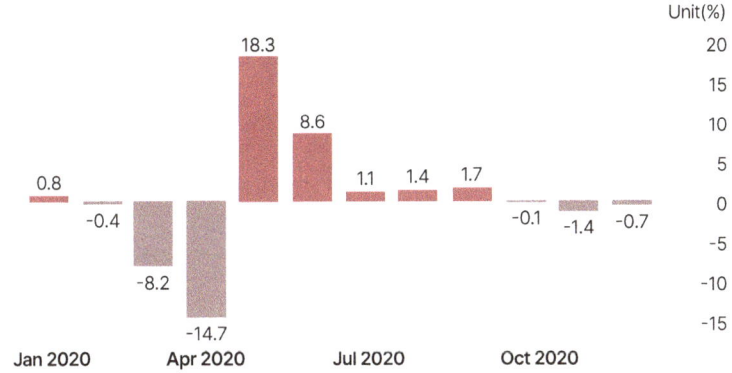

Retail sales increase rate (monthly) in the US

Source: TRADINGECONOMICS.COM | U.S. CENSUS BUREAU

PEPSICO can be said to be a case that quickly responded to the market even in challenging environments, and successfully turned a crisis into an opportunity. Traditionally, the distribution industry has the tendency to be conservative in its strategies, and industrial characteristics that promote rapid change and innovation are difficult to incorporate because agencies and distribution channels are already established. PEPSICO has succeeded despite such traits. Generally, most of the U.S. food distribution goes through B2B agencies. PEPSICO has opened a D2C Direct to Customer channel, to skip the intermediate distribution process and increase the agility of logistics and customer response. In particular, the crisis was turned into an opportunity by setting popular product lines among PEPSICO brands by category, and selling them by themes

PEPSICO sales status

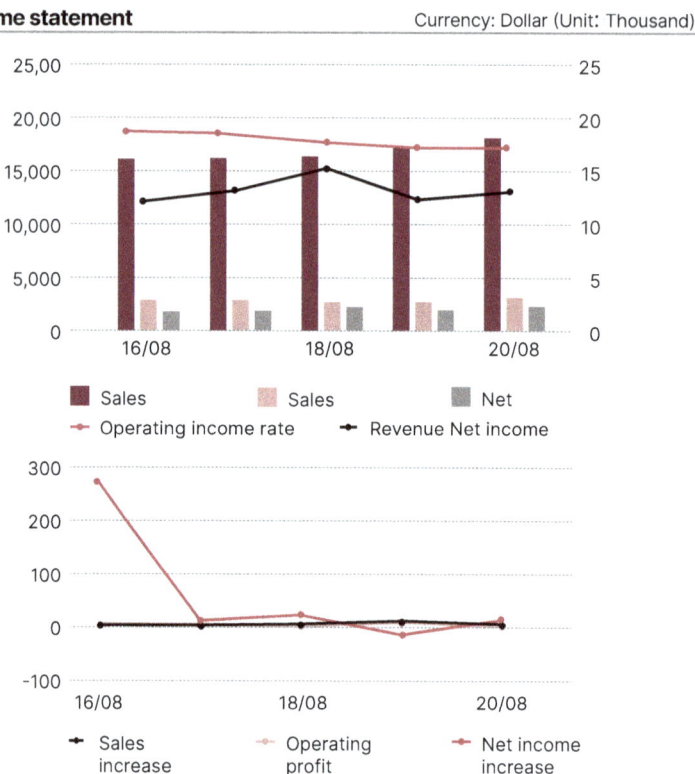

Source: Investing.com

such as snacks, products for breakfast, and products that are good to eat after exercise.

In addition, since the demand for snacks surged during COVID-19, a separate channel was established so that customers could purchase snacks more conveniently through Snacks.com, a subsidiary of PEPSICO. Of course, the increase in sales of groceries may be the reason for the success, but considering PEPSICO is originally a beverage company, this response stands out even more. Amid the COVID-19 crisis, the core of PEPSICO's reaction can be summarized into two main categories.

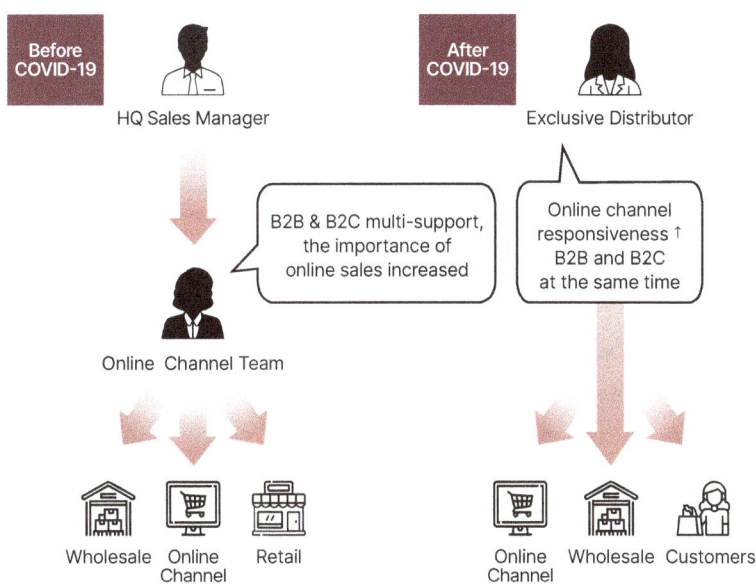

Changes in PEPSICO's way of working

PEPSICO's Success Strategy

1. Changing the way of working: Agile, getting things done quickly

To cope with the New Normal era, PEPSICO established a committee in each division, and held a meeting every two weeks to conduct performance reviews and discussions, to reallocate resources in the division. In particular, while monitoring market changes, customers could participate in decision-making actively. It allowed customer-centered decisions to be made quickly, which is the core of the agile mentality. Through this process, faster market response and pivoting were possible. In general, this change in decision-making is more pronounced, because it is not common for large retailers such as PEPSICO to set business goals and modify business plans at the beginning of the year.

2. Bold investment in new businesses and opportunities

The secret to PEPSICO's achieving results in the New Normal era was that they made bold investments in new opportunities, such as opening new channels and establishing new categories, to strengthen their position in the market, and at the same time, made decisions while closely analyzing cost structures.[10] As a result, even during the pandemic, these bold investments and new attempts brought more successful market responses and dominance than its rival Coca-Cola. In the case of PEPSICO, it is taking a more aggressive strategy to seek growth, and risk management has been efficiently carried out. With the digitization of retail channels, PEPSICO's response is different from that of Coca-Cola, which still relies on existing channels and the beverage market, when the pandemic has brought about consumers' changing consumption patterns (simple meals and drinks at home, not restaurants).

CASE STUDY

[Audi, Hyundai Motor Company]
Online sales through digital consulting

One industry hit hard by COVID-19 in 2020 was the automobile market. This is because production and logistics were blocked by COVID-19, causing difficulties in the global supply chain. And it was not easy to operate at a time when customers could not visit

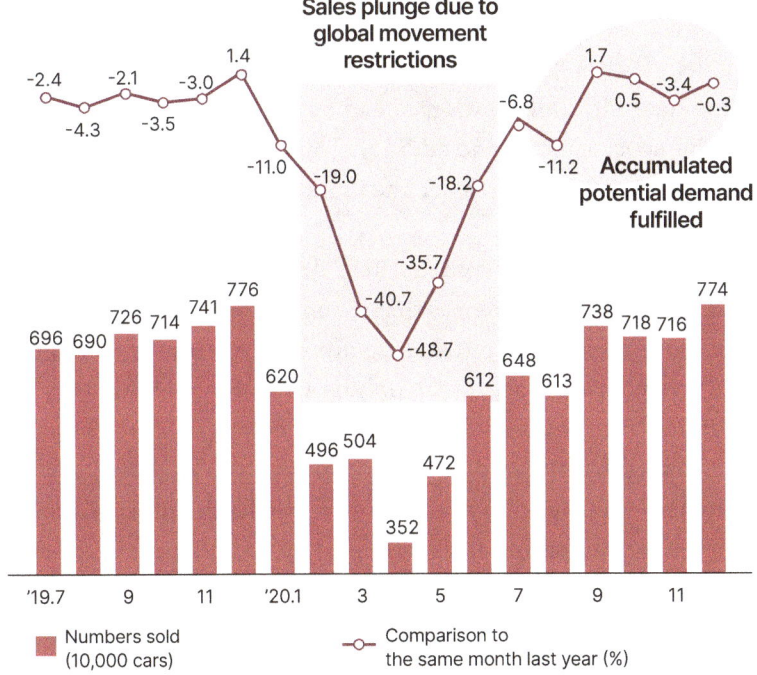

Global car market sales status

Source: Hyundai Motor Group Global Management Research Institute (2021)
https://www.hankyung.com/car/article/202101123271g

29

dealerships or offline stores with these high-involvement products, such as cars.

In particular, sales in the domestic market, as well as the global market, plunged due to the lockdown in European countries.

Against this backdrop, global carmakers such as Audi and Hyundai Motor Company have attempted to switch to online sales. The process of visiting a car dealership and test driving the vehicle or purchasing counseling offline transitioned to online, and digital live consulting using VR devices were introduced to provide experiences such as test-drive. The shopping experience, which was only possible offline, has been converted into a form that can be experienced anywhere. Similar to physically trying out a vehicle, or consulting with the car dealer while looking at the car in person, a sales consultant explains everything online, while looking at the vehicle with a customer wearing data glasses. Customers are provided with information ahead of time on car performance, engine specifications, and additional options for customizing their vehicle, making it even easier and more convenient to obtain information.

Audi also provides virtual test drive services. It indirectly provides testing experiences that are understandably critical to the decision-making and purchasing process. As a result, Audi broke the presumption that cars can only be sold offline because they are high-involvement products. In addition, online sales are gradually increasing, by integrating digital solutions that allow users to purchase vehicles directly online. In particular, in the Chinese market, signed online sales increased by 10,000 units in the first quarter of 2020, 19% higher than the previous year.[11]

Audi also converted to digital when it comes to education for salespeople worldwide, while shifting their sales processes and approaches. Previously, corporations and organizations provided education by fostering professional instructors in each operated region, but during the pandemic, the headquarters provided higher-quality education by conducting live classes online.

Hyundai Motor Company is also proactively engaging in shifting to online sales. Hyundai Motor Company launched "Click to Buy," an online sales platform across the United States and India, starting in April 2020. Hyundai's online sales platform makes the vehicle purchasing process smooth and easy, from getting a quote for a purchase order to delivery of the car.

| Digital consulting between salesperson and customer

* The accompanying pictures are used for illustration purpose only

Audi And Hyundai's Success Strategy

1. Offering customers the same experiences online as offline

What customers want to obtain when purchasing a vehicle is not the vehicle per se, but the experiences gained while driving it. As discussed earlier, Audi and Hyundai proactively offered their customers virtual space experiences similar to offline purchasing, by enabling salespeople to demonstrate and explain the products in person. Both Audi and Hyundai Motor Company made online customers feel the same way they would feel offline.

Before COVID-19, customers had to visit dealerships in person, meet the salespeople, and try out the products, where temporal and spatial issues arose, but now they can consult and test-drive through VR services. They could even physically get a test-drive car to try it out of online sales. Due to the advantages of simplifying these processes and improving customers' convenience, online sales will likely become a new purchasing channel even after the pandemic ends.

| Customers' journey for product purchasing before and after COVID-19

2. A rapid transition to digital consulting & online sales

Audi and Hyundai Motor Company maintained their sales to some extent, through rapid online conversion of the dealership network even during the shutdown period in each country. Traditionally, sales results for automobiles vary depending on the sales capabilities of agents/dealers. Therefore, no matter how well the headquarters try to establish sales strategies, new systems are in vain if each agent/dealer remains unprepared. Both companies responded quickly, so that the headquarters' digital strategy could spread nicely to the field, and that was a critical factor of success.

3. Improving capabilities through digital education

In particular, it should be noted that along with this transition to digital consulting, digital education has been strengthened, so that salespeople familiar with the offline sales process can also be enabled to sell products online. The success of digital transformation was not just carried out for online systems and channels, but also by providing support for salespeople and employees. In the past, separate training was conducted in each operated country or region, by fostering instructors specializing in sales or services. But in the COVID-19 era, it was possible to innovate in terms of expertise, cost and effectiveness, and propagation of know-how and ideas, by reducing intermediate steps and promoting live classes and online education led by headquarters.

CASE STUDY
Digital pivoting: BTS, My Real Trip

One of the industries that faced the most challenges since the outbreak of COVID, was the performance and art industry. This is because there is no way to avoid COVID-19 due to the nature of this industry, where large crowds must gather. Still, there were cases of extraordinary success despite this situation.

BTS and American rapper Travis Scott's stories are definitely among these successful cases. The two singers held online concerts and music video showcases for the Fortnite users worldwide using Metaverse, a virtual reality world. BTS actively responded to the situation by first releasing their "Dynamite" music video to the virtual world, and holding online shows. They set a tremendous record, with three of their songs ranking at the top of the Billboard chart in 2020 alone. Travis Scott also earned 20 billion won by making avatars and performing at Fortnite.

Of course, it cannot be said that they were successful simply because they responded well to the status quo, as they did have a steady fan base even before everything happened. However, both singers managed to create new opportunities by reacting quickly to the changing environment.

Another similar case is My Real Trip, a Korean startup company in the travel industry. It quickly responded to the situation where global travel was impossible due to COVID-19, giving new value to consumers who desired to travel. Like the performance industry, the travel industry had the worst year in 2020. However, My Real Trip took advantage of this situation, and turned it into an opportunity. City tours in various countries, that were previously done offline, were conducted through online live-streaming services, creating an entirely new market.

My Real Trip provides online, live city tours in real-time, at overseas travel destinations. It is an online travel service in which professional guides living abroad visit the travel destinations, directly showing customers the local scenery, and communicating in real-time with virtual tour participants.

BTS, Travis Scott, My Real Trip's Success Strategy

1. Proactive response

Unlike most performing arts companies or singers' passively waiting for strategies, BTS and Travis Scott proactively adopted a methodology that had never been tried before. As a pioneer in adopting a new trend, performing on metaverse can draw good responses from the fans. Even if it failed, it would not be a bad choice when offline performances were primarily limited.

> **Metaverse** This is a compound word of "Universe," and "Meta," which means "after or beyond," and is used to signify change or alteration. Together, the word 'metaverse' points to a three-dimensional, virtual world, and is mainly used as an advanced conceptual terminology.

2. Focusing on the consumer's needs

During the COVID-19 period, consumers spent more time at home due to telecommuting and shutdown, resulting in an increased need for activities they could do at home. In this situation, customers' needs to find new things to watch or play with were bound to increase. Consumers' changing consumption patterns can be seen more clearly by looking at the noticeable growth of OTT services such as Netflix in 2020. New types of performances, such as a concert in a virtual space, can adequately address consumers' complaints and desires and meet their needs. Despite such a rapidly changing consumer consumption pattern, we find a common pattern in several of these successful cases.

Firstly, we need to acknowledge and understand the changing environment caused by COVID-19. Until early 2020, no one predicted that the pandemic would last this long. However, the companies mentioned above properly managed customer changes, trend changes, and daily changes; these could be the driving forces for their success in overcoming the difficulties of COVID-19 compared to other companies.

Secondly, proactive responses cannot be overlooked. The companies mentioned above stood out for their proactive responses and agile approaches. Despite being a distributing company, PEPSICO responded by checking and revising its goals and plans every two weeks to cope with the crisis. It "borrowed" the Agile methodology, initially a methodology used among IT companies, setting up tremendous implications for other companies in the market where rapid responses needed to be made.

Finally, it can be pointed out that the hidden needs of consumers have to be fulfilled somehow. Neither COVID-19 nor the New Normal era means that customers stop consuming, or that their needs disappear. The important thing is to understand what consumers want, and what fans want in this situation. BTS succeeded thanks to understanding and meeting the needs of consumers, who yearned to communicate with singers even in a virtual environment. In this situation, it is necessary to focus more on the needs and inconveniences of consumers.

Now, it's time to change our perceptions

Yes. If you fail to respond appropriately to new changes and fall behind, your survival might be in danger. Like with the previous successful cases, continuous efforts in response to recent changes and trends are needed. As some may say that a crisis is sometimes an opportunity; if you proactively respond to the changes and follow the trend, you will indeed find more opportunities.

Then what should we do first? To begin with, change our perceptions and point of view. As we have seen in the case of change blindness, people are often unaware of minor changes in customers or competitors around them. You might think everything is under control, but the world is changing faster than you think. To escape from this change blindness, it is necessary to get rid of the conventional way of thinking, think outside the box, and learn to think in terms of others' and customers' perspectives.

A shift in perspective is not something complicated. A video became popular on the internet a few years ago. A visually impaired person was asking pedestrians on the street for help and money, and a woman approached and began to write something down on the visually impaired person's sign. The visually impaired person did not know what exactly the woman was doing. However, after the woman revised the written content on the poster, many more people were willing to help. Pedestrians started to donate more money. A few hours later, that woman came back. The visually impaired person asked, out of curiosity, "What did you write?"

"I wrote the same thing. I just put it in different words," the woman answered.

The sentence written previously said, "I am blind. Help me."

The woman had changed the sentence into something like this: "It's a dazzlingly beautiful day. But I can't see it."

The visually impaired person had written the original sign based on their own perspective, while the woman rewrote the sign from the perspective of a seeing person, like most pedestrians who passed by. In that way, the perspective shift began by thinking from the other person's point of view.

Recently, Korea's Taekwondo rules have changed dynamically, another example of changing perspectives. Previously, Taekwondo was challenging to score in; even if the players succeeded in scoring, they tended to be passive in the offense as they tried to keep the score. This made viewers feel bored, so Taekwondo was even excluded from the Asian Games. The general public always had difficulty understanding the final winner's decision-making procedure; with this above-mentioned passive gaming process, Taekwondo barely avoided being kicked out of the Olympics. When watching Taekwondo games, most games become less attractive as the players repeat the same technique: they do a turn kick, and quickly move back when they score. The Taekwondo game, which had always been held the way mentioned above, has changed significantly since 2020. Those who succeed in attacking no longer have to protect their scores. If they succeed in attacking, the opponent's gauge decreases, like in the game Street Fighter. The advantage of this rule is that the game ends only when the opponent's gauge is reduced to the very bottom, so the players are encouraged to attack more actively. The audience can check the players' gauge in real-time, making it easier to keep up with who succeeded in the attack and how the game is going.

In addition, the gauge decreases differently depending on the intensity, area, and technique of the attack, allowing viewers to watch the various courses of action like games. Players who passively play the game will receive a penalty of 20 seconds, which will result in an additional reduction in the gauge if they are attacked during this time. If the game was formerly played from the players' and the game facilitators' perspectives, it is now played keeping the viewer's perspective in mind. Taekwondo has been transformed into a fun and dynamic game that takes its audience into consideration.

    Changing perspectives in such a way is simpler than you might think. In the COVID era, the first thing needed to make the leap from this strategic inflection point is to think from the perspective of other people; of the customers. In the next chapter, we'll take a closer look at the actual changes in sales and businesses, and how these should evolve in the COVID era.

> "The fear that we have, the anxiety that we have, that's not just going to go away. When do we get back to normal? I don't think we get back to normal. I think we get back, or we get to a New Normal. Right? Like we're seeing in so many facets of society right now. So we will be at a different place."

Chapter 2

Sales New Normal #2
Changes in the way you work

In the New Normal era, how should sales departments' work change?

🚩 This is what the former governor of New York, Andrew Cuomo, who was popular in the United States during the COVID-19 pandemic, said at a regular briefing. Indeed, even if COVID-19 fully goes away someday, we will not be able to return to the world as it was before. Only people and organizations who adapt quickly to the new normal can survive the whirlwind of change.

Then, let's take a look at the changes caused by COVID-19. For individuals, their daily lives have changed a lot. Working remotely has become familiar, online consumption has soared due to the trend of contact-free services, and demand for online education has also increased significantly. As gatherings reduced, solitary hobbies naturally began to gain popularity. And the changes are not limited to individuals: COVID-19 is also bringing forth many changes for companies. The biggest concern would be productivity. Working remotely, as in working from home instead of the office, leads to concerns about work efficiency. Managers became anxious, as there were some difficulties in monitoring and controlling whether their employees worked hard or not. From the employees' perspective, it is also a problem that the boundaries between work and life are collapsing. Given the situation mentioned above, companies are wondering how to adapt their way of working in response to the changing environment. The sales department and the HR department have been hard at work, trying to figure out how to deliver results differently than before.

How will the post-COVID era change the way salespeople work? Let's take a look at some real-life examples.

CASE STORY 1

Salespeople are in danger due to COVID-19

* The story is based on a real-life incident, and some details/information have been adapted.

K, a department manager of Company A, a domestic medical equipment manufacturing company, has had difficulty continuing his work as usual during the COVID era. Before COVID-19, K traveled worldwide and had a busy schedule attending overseas exhibitions and conferences, visiting overseas dealers, and doing equipment demonstrations. In particular, K knew the equipment reasonably well, making K an exceptional talent for offline sales procedures, such as visiting customers in-person to solve simple technical problems. As a result, K successfully built a trust-based long-term relationship with their customers. And K's working network was undoubtedly the best in the industry, in the regions of the Americas.

However, with the outbreak of COVID-19, K's way of working has reached its limit. For instance, overseas exhibitions have been wholly canceled, and overseas business trips have been restricted. There is no way to care for existing customers, and it has become challenging to create new customers. Conferences and equipment demonstrations are being held, to receive inquiries from new customers and establish a social network, but these opportunities have been blocked due to COVID-19. Instead, as all conferences were conducted online, new competencies not required in the past, like handling video shooting equipment and operating online live classes, are now in need. Holding online conference calls with customers was already challenging; providing the customers with the same quality of services as an offline visit was harder. Therefore, even if minor mistakes occurred, such as technical problems, the reputation would be potentially harmed. Furthermore, as COVID-19, expected to end quickly, was rampant for a long time, difficulties continued to increase.

K. thought he could show his strengths again when COVID ends, at least in the second half of 2020. Still, the situation only worsened since he did not pay much attention to the use of online meeting tools or other online exhibition activities.

Not only K., but his boss J. as well, the sales team leader, complains of insomnia due to severe stress during the COVID era. Aside from falling sales, the lack of customer management has also intensified competition, increasing J's stress levels. On top of that, sales departments are greatly affected by short-term performance, and the vibe of these organizations could be easily changed according to the external business environment; the overall atmosphere was stagnant. When salespeople, accustomed to meeting customers face-to-face, feel anxious and frustrated because they cannot go outside, their concerns about the organization's operation start to deepen. Moreover, even if COVID-19 ends, there are predictions everywhere that offline operations will take more time to recover fully. Overall, it is time to change the way things work.

The situation above has been happening in many business organizations since COVID-19 hit. According to an interview with a global pharmaceutical company's sales department, sales are being replaced by contact-free online conference calls. Product demonstrations and conferences are gradually being replaced by webinars. As mentioned earlier, salespeople's roles, competencies, and strategies to approach customers are also changing during this process. Global electronics and car manufacturing companies are also focusing on product-training-related content production and online sales consulting activities, to strengthen online sales following the shutdown of offline stores.[1]

Change 1: Switching from offline to digital

According to a survey of 3,600 B2B sales decision-makers around the world conducted by global consulting firm McKinsey, the critical changes in corporate management after COVID-19 can be summarized into three main categories.

First, there is an expected decrease in the budget. As businesses face more and more operational challenges, the budget is expected to be relatively reduced compared to before COVID-19. The second change is the digital transformation of both the working and working channels. The transition to digital has been underway since before COVID-19; as COVID-19 accelerated the pace of change, it has become an irreversible trend. The third is remote selling. Like other departments, since the sales department is also experiencing difficulties meeting their customers offline due to remote working and social distancing, the importance of remote selling is naturally emerging.

According to the survey results regarding post-COVID-19 sales activities, leaders of B2B companies believe that sales activities and interactions through digital channels are about twice as important to customers as traditional offline-based sales.

In addition, although it varies from country to country, about 90% of sales channels have already shifted to video conferences, phone calls, and web-based sales models. In Korea, which has proactively responded to the changing environment, about 60% of them are conducting wholly or partially remote operations. Of course, some skepticism remains, but more than half of the respondents said that remote selling would deliver the same or even better results compared to the sales approach before COVID-19.[2]

As seen from the figure on the right, before COVID-19, offline channels such as in-person sales, exhibitions, and conferences accounted for the most frequent way of approaching and managing customers.

On the other hand, in the post-COVID era, customer follow-ups through online channels such as webinars, homepages, and social media are expected to become more critical than face-to-face sales such as in-person visits, exhibitions, and conferences. Those essential decisions were made offline in the past, through exhibitions or face-to-face meetings. Online sales will become more critical in the post-COVID era, where salespeople receive customer inquiries, identify customer needs, and propose solutions for customers through digital channels.

In the future, changes will accelerate further, and as with B2C sales channels, obtaining information through websites, blogs, and YouTube channels will become more critical. Salespeople should cooperate more closely with the marketing department, so that customers can effectively get and inquire about information from these channels. Thus, when thinking about UX (User Experience), it is necessary to consider the changes related to B2B channels.

The change in the importance of B2B customer sales channels after COVID-19

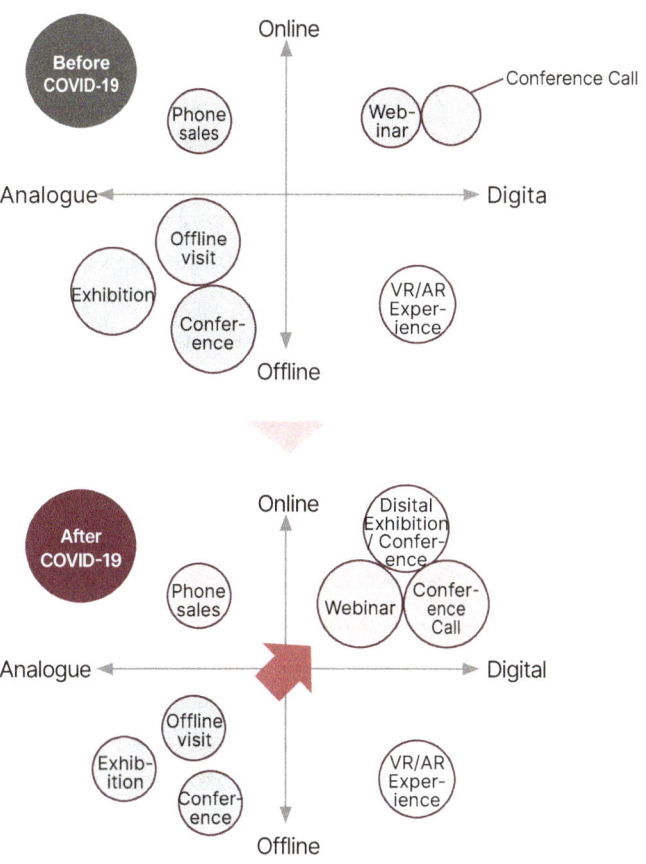

* The size of a circle means frequency and importance

In recent years, face-to-face exhibitions have been converted into virtual exhibitions. More and more companies have made VR exhibition halls to conduct businesses or shift offline activities to online, through holding online engagement marketing activities and events on the Zoom platform.

The scene on the right page is a part of an online conference in which Hyundai Motor Company's annual offline conference is organized into a virtual space, introducing new products to experts and partners from each country, and conducting sales activities and product training.

The event, which used to be held offline in the past, was organized as a virtual conference in January this year by integrating product education, sales, and service training, to introduce new cars and share information such as company strategies and policies for dealers around the world. Escaping from the one-way information delivery methodology, this event even served as a knowledge-sharing venue for learners worldwide to share their best practices and exchange opinions. In the past, offline conferences had advantages in forming networks between learners, but there were also limitations. However, since Hyundai Motor Company recently introduced virtual spaces like online exhibitions, participants' experiences have been optimized by building several virtual booths and providing content that considered the differences in competencies and localization. In addition, since not everyone can participate in offline events due to time and space constraints, online community activities in which more people share information in virtual spaces were strengthened.

After COVID-19, many companies experienced cost reduction and the advantages of online sales as they digitized the way they work, in particular at their sales department. Now it is time to think based on online sales activities instead of offline. It is true that the

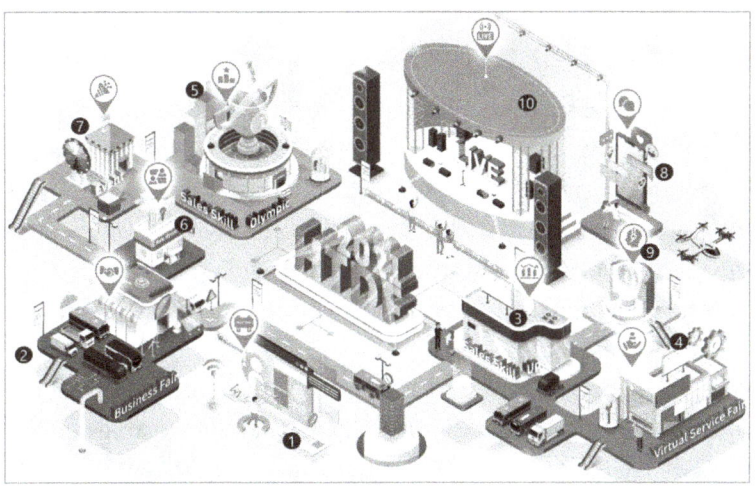

Virtual Space Composition
❶ Welcome Board ❷ Business Fair (ex. Introduction of new products)
❸ Sales skill up (Sales training zone)
❹ Service skill up (Service training zone)
❺ Sales sill Olympics (Best Practice sharing) ❻ Ask Hyundai
❼ Event (Gamification) ❽ Small talk (Community) ❾ Help Desk
❿ Live Session

Source : Pandemic in HRD department is a crisis and opportunity,
DBR February 2021 Issue. 1

company managers we have worked with, including the above mentioned event, were worried about online sales activities and exhibitions at first, but now they have started to see online activities positively. Of course, online sales activities cannot always be suitable, and offline activities cannot be 100% replaced. Depending on the situation and case, it will be necessary to respond flexibly.

Change 2: Increased importance of data and information distribution

According to a survey conducted by Business 2 Community, a U.S. sales specialized content agency, 73.9% of B2B sales managers responded that they were losing sales opportunities due to COVID-19. Does this mean that all sales opportunities have disappeared? No. In fact, 26.1% of sales representatives said they were getting new sales opportunities.[3] Why does this difference occur, and how should we respond?

Let's go back to K's case. K. was a salesperson with a skillset and strengths in offline sales services. Not only has his existing network already been established in the past, but K. has also professional knowledge of the products, and well-managed relationships with the customers. One disadvantage was that he lacked the ability to utilize data. As a typical salesman, K. has increased sales by discovering customers' hidden needs through his relationship-oriented personality and unique communication skills. However, this ability shines the most when face-to-face sales are possible. Since he was not recording or managing sales data properly after conducting customer meetings and exhibitions, it was not easy to create new opportunities other than managing his existing customer relationships after COVID-19.

But let's suppose for a second that K. had done a good job managing the data of the customers he had a meeting with, or the customers who decided to opt-out from the purchase at the decision-making stage. In that case, the data could have been utilized, and become a new opportunity when non-face-to-face sales approaches are needed after COVID-19. If so, K. could have fully demonstrated his strengths during online sales as he did offline. This is because if K. held online meetings by identifying customers' preferences and needs in detail based on the records, close customer

Pros and cons of existing conferences and online conferences

Clasification	Existing conferences	Online conferences
Place / Number of participants	• It's conducted in a specific region • Only a few people from HQ could attend	• Corporates/agents/dealership representatives from all around the world attend in virtual space
Event composition / contents	• Business direction, New product launching show • Part of the product training process • Network of attendees by region	• Live event (introduction of new products, business direction) • Skills Olympics (*BP sharing) * BP : Best Practice • Sales, Service Skills Training (Level Up) • Community operation, product training
Strengths	• Offline events, social networking is easy • High level of immersion	• No restrictions on time and place. • Reduce event costs (transportation, moving, accommodation, etc.) • Easy to share and spread knowledge and content. • Differentiated contents can be provided by level and region • Various human resources can participate. • Low language barrier (utilized automatic translation system, TTS, etc.)

relationships—like those in offline sales—could be formed and managed.

However, many sales departments, like K's, rely only on salespeople's senses, and fail to capture the data of their selling procedures. According to a study of B2B companies in the United States, about 44% of the leaders said their organizations were not correctly managing the data of their sales pipeline.4 In particular, large sales departments and teams targeting global markets will have no choice but to rely on their salespeople's senses if they fail to monitor which customers they met and what activities they did.

In the case mentioned above, data utilization is obviously at a lower level, making it difficult for organizations to focus on sales or important customers that need to be well-managed. In addition, there are cases where demands for R&D or support departments are left out. Also, it becomes more challenging to master the DB for existing and potential customers, and determine who should be targeted. These procedures are far from systematic and strategic.

The B2B sales pipeline is generally shown in the figure. The sales process must be tracked and managed at each stage, and data should be accumulated and available across the entire pipeline. Customers must be systematically managed at each stage of potential customer pool management, from needs analysis, to proposals and negotiations, to the actual sales closing, and customer follow-ups. The pipeline is not an entirely new concept. Perhaps you remember from your school chemistry class, that the entrance of a funnel is large, and it becomes narrower as it goes down. Like the funnel, the method of gradually obtaining the final output step by step is called pipeline management. And the output coming through a series of processes is the closing of the sale.

B2B sales pipeline

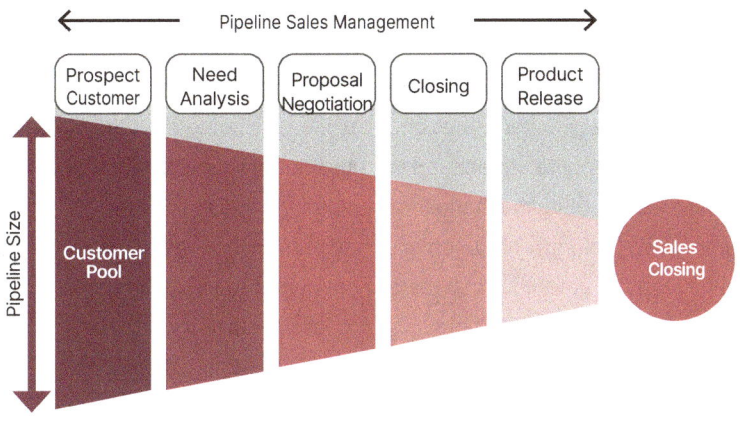

The Stages of The Sales Pipeline

1. Potential Customer Pool Management^{Lead Qualification}

This is the stage where sales opportunities are being evaluated. Sales consultants should understand the business status of their potential customers, that is, the market and industry to which potential customers belong, and determine their primary needs accordingly. If the evaluation of potential customers is not done properly, sales consultants can waste unnecessary time targeting less important customers, or customers who are less likely to lead to successful sales results. Therefore, managing and analyzing potential customers is essential. At the same time, we must ensure and secure as many customer pools as possible. This may sound obvious, but in the end, only an extensive collection of potential customers can increase the total sales volume.

2. Needs Analysis^{Engagement}

At this stage, meetings are held, to visit potential customers or identify their needs.

3. Proposal Negotiation^{Solution}

This is the stage of proposing to customers a solution to fulfill their needs or solve their problems, both of which should have been determined in the previous step. At this stage, proposal presentations or negotiations are sometimes conducted, to talk customers into the project.

4. Closing^{Close a deal}

At this stage, customers are convinced to purchase, and contracts, product release preparations, and the final release are made after the purchase is confirmed.

> **Information that must be entered into the sales pipeline**
>
> - Product Information: Goods, Other Services
> - Potential Sales for Future Opportunities: the expected monetary value the customers will create
> - Expected Closing Time: Depending on the customer's decisions, it is the time when a sales opportunity is fulfilled, realized, or closed
> - Sales Phase: Pipeline Phases Designed by a Company
> - Estimated Sales Potential: The Success Probability of a Company's Potential Sales
> - Customer Representatives: The client company representatives in charge of purchasing influence the purchase decisions.
> - Customer Requirements: Specific Requirements for Products and Services
> - Sales Channels: Sales Channels where products and services are sold
> - Sales Opportunity Inflow channels: Channels that have created sales opportunities

According to a survey by Jason Jordan and Robert Kelly of the American Sales Management Association, companies that manage sales through the sales pipeline have 15% higher sales than those that do not.5 In particular, companies that organize their sales processes, manage the sales pipeline, and review each phase showed a 28% increase in their sales results. It is a significant difference that sales increase by about 30% simply through reviewing and managing sales results, by utilizing the data of the sales pipeline. The difference is even more remarkable considering how much salespeople usually strive to grow even 10% of sales.

In this way, using data in sales management is very efficient. In addition, through the sales pipeline one can more effectively determine what customers want at each stage, what obstacles make them unable to go to the next step, and what support and help other departments need to offer.

The use of data was an important issue, even before COVID-19. Still, particularly in the post-COVID era, a customer who needs to be confirmed by the marketing department must be followed up properly, without omission by the sales department; as shown below, close collaboration and response between departments have become more critical. Above all, when offline customer experience shifts to online, customer management through more detailed,

| Customer purchasing process

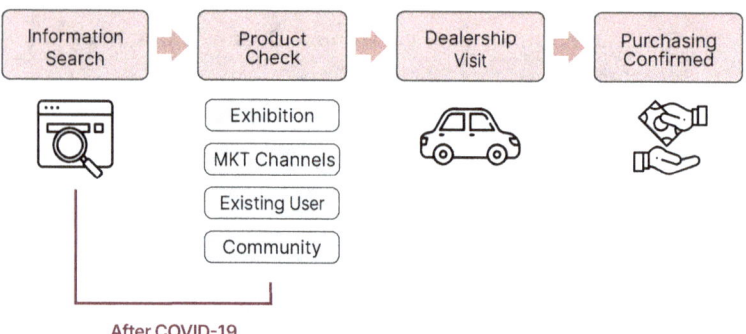

After COVID-19
It is essential that data is accumulated and managed through the sales pipeline

customer-centered thinking, and data management and utilization should be simultaneously carried out.

Moreover, as seen in the online exhibition and digitalization cases we looked at earlier, securing, analyzing, and utilizing data online are decisive factors in sales success. This is why we should pay more attention to data in the post-COVID era.

Change 3: Changes in the way salespeople work

The following is a partial adaptation of the interview with the sales team leader J, the main character of the previous case.

> **The Writer** What's the most significant change after COVID-19?
>
> **Team Leader J** The most significant difference is that the salesperson's competencies and capabilities are clearly shown and highlighted.
>
> **The Writer** Given the limitation of the offline sales activities, how did you pinpoint the differences?
>
> **Team Leader J** First, it was difficult to check these in detail, because everyone was engaged in offline sales. Since we're doing a lot of online sales activities, it's easier to check how many sales activities salespeople are doing, and how they conduct their work at the headquarters. These differences in activities are also shown as achievements. And in some regions, sales remain unchanged, even though there is less contact with customers due to restrictions on offline activities. This brings the need of our existence into question, and is a challenge for our team.
>
> **The Writer** I see how that can be an issue.
>
> **Team Leader J** And as we conduct conference calls and webinars, each salesperson shows different skills. Salespeople who are more familiar with these tools will have more advantages. This

difference leads to more sales opportunities, and of course, a difference in results.

The Writer What other issues are there?

Team Leader J There is a significant difference between offline meetings and conference calls. In the case of conference calls, the emotions and connections felt offline are excluded. Instead, expertise is highlighted, and it becomes essential to deliver accurate information within a short period of time. Salespeople even pay more attention to how they look on the screen, their clothes, and their attitude. It's an environment where salespeople focus more on their appearance than in offline sales, and where establishing trust during the process is essential.

The Writer There's been a significant change in the way you work. It must be hard.

Team Leader J Yes, I miss the times before COVID-19. Learning new skills is also time-consuming. Oh, there's one good thing: it's good to save time and money by reducing business trips. But of course, that could be more stressful for salespeople.

As we can see from the interview above, the competencies and ways of working for salespeople are rapidly changing as face-to-face and offline sales decrease. Identifying customer needs, and offering product-related information, are the most critical competencies of salespeople, which will remain unchanged whether offline or online. However, in the post-COVID era, the product information must be delivered clearly in a shorter time, as it is carried out online instead of offline. If a product demonstration is conducted, the ability to handle equipment and relevant skills will also become very important, so that the product can be well-demonstrated in an online-based environment. In addition, as mentioned above, as sales and product expertise become more prominent, salespeople will need to possess more professional knowledge, attitude, and skills than relationship-oriented sales in the past. In terms of information delivery, since online has more restrictions than offline, changes are also required in the contents of the information. Let's look at some of these changes in how we work in more detail.

First, it is necessary to change the sales preparation and process. In the past, during offline sales, salespeople presented brochures, or prepared materials face-to-face to customers. They allowed customers to experience the equipment directly, or they demonstrated the product by operating it. However, these activities must be prepared more carefully in advance for online sales. First of all, you have to decide which tool to use. For small conference calls, holding sales meetings and explaining prepared materials in real-time, using video conferencing tools such as Zoom and Teams will be more effective. However, a webinar using YouTube live streaming might be more efficient for a product demonstration, or a large conference. This is because using tools such as screen sharing is more suitable for live broadcasting. In this case, it is recommended to pre-record product demonstration and introduction videos, to prevent possible mishaps and emphasize expertise. Since during online non-face-to-face sales, even small mistakes such as behaviors, intonation, and skills in handling products are highlighted, salespeople's expertise is regarded as more critical. And when a webinar is conducted, instead of responding to the participants' requirements alone by the sales team, it is better to incorporate the help of departments such as technical support and R&D teams to quickly respond to customer or technical inquiries. In addition, since constantly checking the client company's reactions and responses are relatively limited, asking questions proactively or having Q&A sessions slotted in, is important in order to encourage customers to participate.

The second is the change in content. In the past, brochures and company introduction materials produced by the marketing team were often standardized and used across the process. These materials were made for offline sales, and online non-face-to-face sales require customized content to suit the user's situation. Since online explanation usually takes a shorter time than offline procedures, when designing an online educational curriculum, sales representatives should be able to increase customer concentration by preparing content that participants can understand more quickly, as well as related video materials to support the developed content. And after the meeting, it is necessary to provide materials and recorded videos used during sessions to help customers obtain more detailed information. Also, the form of content should be provided for easier understanding, such as educational content or explanatory materials for B2C customers. In other words, a salesperson should also take on the role of a marketer, producing and providing the content.

In the case of Samsung Electronics, tech seminars originally held offline with customers in each operated region were converted to online tech seminars after COVID-19, to answer client companies' product-related questions and conduct sales without facing them. In addition, after the workshop, this content was turned into, and distributed as, educational material. After COVID-19, sales-related activities do not just end with sales activities per se, but it has become more critical to help customers gain more information about products and services.

Change 4: The role and necessary competencies of the sales department

So far, we have examined how the working methods of salespeople have changed in the COVID era. The most significant change was digitalization, data utilization, and specific changes in working practices. Now, let's find out what competencies salespeople need in response to the changing way of working, and how to polish and develop these skills.

Digital transformation became the hottest topic in 2020. It had been gradually progressing over the years, but advanced rapidly due to COVID-19. People even joke that what ushered in DT was not a CEO or CTO, but COVID-19.

Amid this changing trend, salespeople should play the role of a change agent who actively accepts and leads the digital transformation. A change agent is an individual or a group supporting and influencing organizational changes. For example, suppose the COVID era is when online sales should be actively introduced and examined. As change agents, salespeople should learn various skills, and develop their online sales competencies daily. In an era where change is accelerating fast, as change agents, salespeople must take the lead to inform and spread the trend across the entire organization.

To spearhead change, salespeople must learn to sell online as soon as possible. The leading role could then be preoccupied with actively utilizing the know-how generated in the process, and spreading it to other departments. As mentioned earlier, the sales department was the first department that needed a transformation due to rapid changes. Now, they will be ready to lead the structural and constitutional improvement and changes.

In 2020, many companies' digital transformation proceeded naturally due to COVID-19, but their competencies are still insufficient. According to a digital agility indicator surveyed by Workday, a company specializing in HR systems, 72% of Korean companies said digital transformation is their top priority. Still, only 3% of employees said they realized digital agility.[6]

People in charge of sales have probably been thinking about digital transformation for a long time. In addition, after COVID-19, it would have been necessary to promote various sales activities

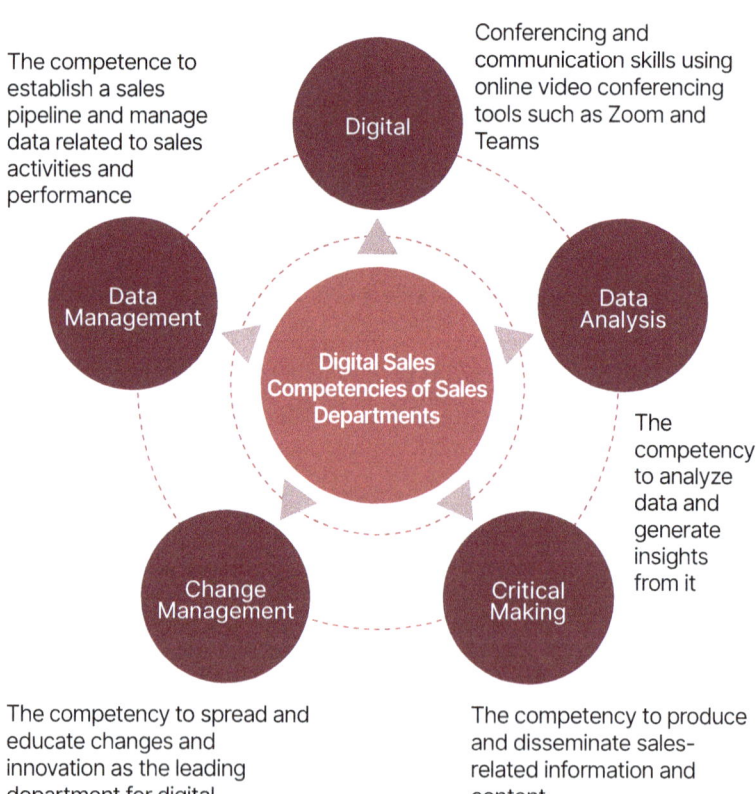

Digital sales competencies of sales departments needed in the COVID era

and content-development-related know-how across the organization using Zoom, Webex, and Teams. As such, the sales team must play a leading role in spreading the necessary digital competencies in the COVID era. So, what digital competencies should salespeople be fitted within the post-COVID era?

Five competencies can be selected: digital communication, data management and utilization, data analysis, content production/utilization, and change management.

First, Data management/utilization competency

As we have seen earlier, this refers to the competency to establish a sales pipeline, record sales results, and manage customer-related information and sales performance data. It is the most fundamental competency, and even before COVID-19, the ability to manage sales data was a core one. We must especially pay more attention to this competency, because performance can vary depending on how data is defined, classified, and managed.

Second, Digital communication competency

Digital communication competency refers to conferencing and communication skills, using online video conferencing tools such as Zoom and Teams. In particular, video conferencing tools may vary depending on customers, so salespeople need to understand these various tools and how to use them better than their customers do. Here, instead of explaining the tools, I would like to introduce a few points to be aware of when conducting online video sales. The Internet, and other referencing books, have a lot of information on how to use these various tools; it's easy to read an article or watch a tutorial and learn the know-how. Therefore, I would like to explain how to proceed with online video sales instead of going through the tools per se.

Sales video conference skills tip

1. When conducting a video conference, the background color should be simple, or virtual background functions offered by Zoom and Teams should be utilized so that the other party can focus on the video conference per se.

2. Since sales deal with customers, even a detail can not be overlooked. Thus, video conferences should be held in a quiet space. Often, there are cases where video conferences are held at cafes due to a lack of suitable places. Still, if possible, video conferences should be conducted in a quiet environment (such as conference rooms or passenger seats of cars).

3. Use earphones or headsets with microphone functions. If you use a PC built-in microphone and speaker, it is recommended to prepare supportive equipment since the sound from the speaker enters the microphone, and the sound might echo.

4. You should pay attention to the lighting when conducting digital communication. If the light is above you, you might leave a bad impression on your customers since your face will be shaded. If possible, setting up the light in front of the face is recommended, making it look brighter. Since lighting is one of the most important things during digital communication, salespeople should pay special attention to it during video conferences with their customers.

5. Another thing you should pay attention to during video conferences is the height of your laptop. Generally speaking, if a laptop is placed on a regular desk, your eyes will look from top to bottom, making a bad

> impression on customers. Thus, it is important to adjust the eye level to the camera level of the laptop or PC. And it's better to look at the lens of the laptop or PC than the screen.
>
> 6. The attire and surrounding environment could be overlooked during online video sales meetings. However, salespeople should pay extra attention to what they are wearing and how they look, especially during video conferences. This is because customers will evaluate the salespeople only according to their appearance and intonation shortly shown in the video conferences. Though these are also important for offline meetings, the impact is greater for online meetings since salespeople are only evaluated by what they showed during the video conferences.

Third, Data analysis competency

This refers to the competency to analyze accumulated data and generate insights from it. For instance, the ability to analyze various data from management systems such as CRM$^{\text{Customer Relationship Management}}$, VOC$^{\text{Voice of the Customer}}$, and GIS$^{\text{Geographic Information System}}$ data, and utilize them for sales. Data analysis was already crucial before COVID-19. But, as online sales activities increased during the COVID era, obtaining new directions and insights from that data has become more important.

Fourth, Content production/utilization competency

In the post-COVID era, producing and utilizing content becomes more critical for salespeople. This is because explanatory materials such as presentations are more often produced and used than before, since what needs to be explained to customers offline is conducted through online digital platforms. In addition, offline meetings have certain restrictions; creating and delivering content such as newsletters for periodically communicating with customers has become vital. In particular, in the case of technology sales, product training is sometimes required, and product training materials should also be created.

In the past, salespeople would directly demonstrate the products and answer any customer questions about them. Now it is more critical to provide the customers or dealerships with a guide to operating the product, allowing them to learn and master the product independently. Therefore, salespeople must more actively improve their ability to create and produce different types of content.

Fortunately, many content production tools have recently come out to help create various content, even if you are not a designer. Some global companies used the content production tools described above to produce their product introduction materials. With a small learning curve, salespeople can also quickly create customized introductions or product training materials without the help of designers. Besides the tools mentioned above, various design tools such as Mango Board are widely used these days, so it is necessary to choose at least one best fit to familiarize yourself with.

Maybe some people think, "This is something a marketer or designer should do, and I don't have to deal with it." However, in the post-COVID era, boundaries in the industry will fade away. In order to survive, salespeople must also break away from a passive position by stepping out of their comfort zone, and developing capabilities of comprehensive thinking to become more competitive.

Content production tools

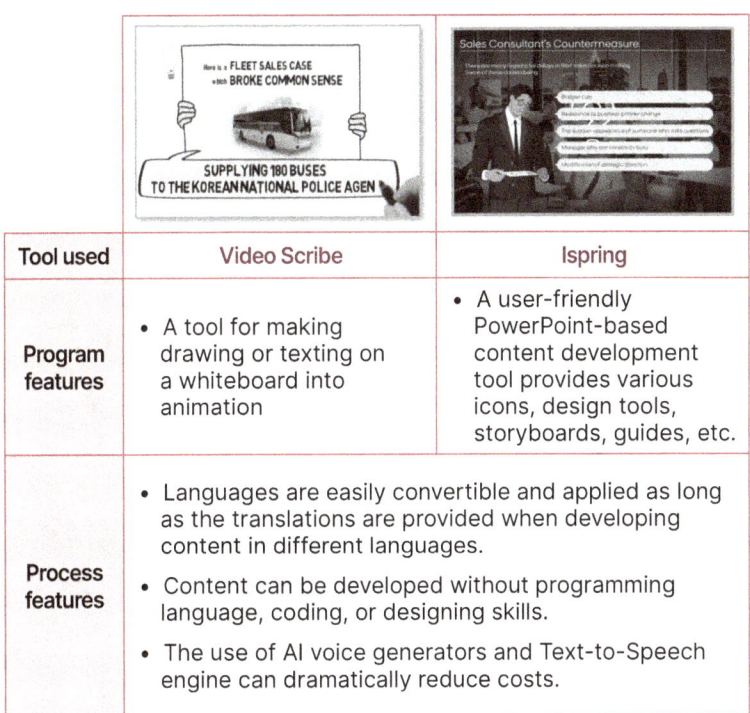

Tool used	Video Scribe	Ispring
Program features	• A tool for making drawing or texting on a whiteboard into animation	• A user-friendly PowerPoint-based content development tool provides various icons, design tools, storyboards, guides, etc.
Process features		• Languages are easily convertible and applied as long as the translations are provided when developing content in different languages. • Content can be developed without programming language, coding, or designing skills. • The use of AI voice generators and Text-to-Speech engine can dramatically reduce costs.

Fifth, Change management

Many things are changing and will continue to change due to COVID-19. Salespeople have already noticed the changing environment, and have started to lead the change. Under these circumstances, developing the competency to accept changes, allow the changes to transform you, and spread the gospel of change is crucial.

There will be salespeople who have already been equipped with the five competencies mentioned above, or there may be salespeople who feel that those competencies are somewhat different from the competencies that they previously thought were necessary. The core of change and competency development relies on the salespeople themselves. Therefore, salespeople should understand the timing of change, discover the competencies they need, and make changes little by little.

CHECKLIST

Post-COVID era, sales department diagnosis table

Category	Checklist
Digital transformation	☐ Is our department preparing for or shifting from offline to digital sales?
	☐ Are channels built to help customers quickly access information?
Data utilization	☐ Are digital channel customer activities, and inquiries analyzed and delivered to the sales department?
	☐ Is the sales pipeline and CRM established to ensure the information flow?
Changes in the way you work	☐ Are salespeople familiar with the tools for non-face-to-face sales? Is adequate education being provided?
	☐ Does the sales department have its principles and standards for customer-approaching strategies and methods suitable for non-face-to-face sales?
	☐ Does the sales department effectively collaborate with the marketing and technical support teams to produce content?
Roles and competencies	☐ Is the sales department leading the changes and playing the role of a change agent?
	☐ Is the sales department equipped with the five necessary competencies?

* The last part of each chapter comprises diagnostic tools to identify and check whether sales departments, leaders, and members respond appropriately to the Sales New Normal era in terms of how they work, performance management, operations of the department, and change management. Following the checklist, we can diagnose and evaluate whether our organization is adapting decently to the changing era.

Chapter 3

Sales New Normal #3
Changes in performance management

In the New Normal era, what is the key to sales departments' performance management?

▎ Many organizations face conflicts between their sales and HR or strategy departments. These conflicts arise from differences in perspectives. Some HR and strategy departments tend to regard the sales departments as the targets for managerial and governing procedures, and salespeople as not to be trusted. Therefore, it is common to manage sales activities with various performance indicators. On the other hand, the sales departments complain, saying, "Sales are a department that should be judged on performance, but the managerial departments take unnecessary initiatives and measure the wrong things during the process."

Suppose you follow the perspectives of the HR and strategy departments. In that case, you will be buried in metrics and evaluation data instead of focusing on the nature of the process or the original goal, causing various problems. Moreover, due to COVID-19, issues related to indicators and metrics are becoming more prominent. As social distancing has been reinforced, and overseas business trips have been restricted, organizations are still viewing similar managerial procedures as before, saying things like "Is the sales department working appropriately?" "They don't seem to be doing anything special, but why are the sales similar as before?" "How should we measure and manage sales?" As offline sales opportunities have reduced, sales departments strive to achieve their goals by changing how they work. As the perspectives and thoughts regarding these situations differ, distrust among departments is bound to deepen. In particular, companies whose performance has not fallen significantly despite COVID-19 are coming up with responses like, "There is no difference in the sales revenue. even though sales activities have reduced." As a result, concerns about how to measure business performance or outcomes are intensifying.

At this point, we need to consider the following: Are the indicators that measure the sales departments working properly? And how should we diagnose and give feedback on the sales departments' activities if we have to work differently than before? In the COVID era, it is necessary to consider whether the sales department should be controlled and managed based on existing perspectives, as work is becoming more personalized and autonomy is being emphasized due to the increase of remote working and selling. Then, let's see how we establish the performance indicators for sales departments, and what issues need to be solved, through examples.

CASE STORY 2

Errors in performance indicators and goals

* The story is based on an actual case, and some details/information have bee adapted.

Kim is a salesperson of Company C, who sells medical equipment to hospitals. Company C recently issued a policy that mandates that customer visits need to happen four times daily. As a result, Kim is busy running back and forth in downtown Seoul all day. The problem is that customer visits do not directly lead to sales revenue.

Moreover, in this COVID era, it is not easy to visit customers four times a day. Because Kim's primary customers are large hospitals, marketing activities that manage the existing customers and secure new customers are considered more effective than visiting random customers. In addition, current customers frequently call in for equipment inspection or hospital-related matters, and it is not easy to refuse them or even have time to visit other places or customers. Kim's situation is somewhat better. In the case of Manager Lee, it was common to be caught up in one place all day long if customers had problems operating their equipment.

As the company unilaterally included the number of customer visits

Strategic tasks	Detailed tasks to achieve performance goals	KPI (Key Performance Indicators)			Weighting
		KPI	Property	KPI formula	
Sales growth for existing customers	Increase sales of major customers through customer and partner management	Total sales goal achievement rate	Quantitative	Goal achievement rate	40%
Achieving the goal of generating sales profits	Increase profits by promoting sales of new products	New product sales target achievement rate	Quantitative	Goal achievement rate	20%
Customer management	Management of the number of customer visits	Daily customer visit target achievement rate	Quantitative	Customer visit goal achievement rate	30%
Management of distressed debt and SG&A expenses	Sales processing (collection, etc.)	Collection rate (%)	Quantitative	Customer visit goal achievement rate	10%

* This is the KPI of Company C's assistant manager Kim, and some modifications/edits have been made due to confidentiality reasons.

in the KPI, they both made meaningless customer visits or entered fake visiting records. This is because the indicator to visit customers has become a factor influencing not only compensation, but also the allocation of sales and marketing costs. As a result, it has become an indicator that salespeople must manage, even with false or fake record entries.

Kim and other team members protested to the sales team leader that it was a ridiculous performance indicator when setting the KPI. Still, the leader did not accept their opinion and reprimanded them, saying, "If the company asks us to do it, we should just do it. Let's not make a fuss or trouble during this difficult time." The following reasons were given for the creation of these performance indicators: as a strategic managerial task, 'improving the performance indicators' is required; and the HR and strategy departments selected the number of daily customer visits applied by other healthcare industries as a major indicator. In the case of other companies, high performers regularly visit customers. When customer visits were set as a quantitative indicator, it was easy to manage salespeople and increase their performance. People argued that Kim's company would also achieve better results if they applied the same performance indicator. Of course, periodic customer visits can create new opportunities; and frequent visits will also help reinforce the customer management for existing customers.

However, in Company C's case, since the product price is high, targeting customers and demonstrating equipment or providing proper consultation when visiting was more likely to lead to sales than visiting customers uncritically. Therefore, salespeople thought that the changed performance indicators aimed not to improve performance, but to evaluate, manage, and control them. In addition, they said that they felt unmotivated and monitored since they had to work while making up false records. Moreover, the frustration doubled as the current performance indicators did not seem to reflect the current situation due to COVID-19 properly. Of course, it is understandable that the company also has its stance. It is not easy to alter decisions, once made by large organizations —especially since measurement indicators are directly connected with the performance evaluation. Kim complained to the seniors on the same team.

"Will the sales go up just because we visit the customers often? These days, the hospital chiefs aren't even easy to meet... It's frustrating."

The seniors answered, "Hey, don't worry. This situation will fade away in a couple of years. COVID-19 is not over yet, so just be careful and hang in there. Why are you so worried? You only have to fill in the number for the KPI. Just make up the sales record. There's nothing else you could do."

After talking with the seniors, Kim felt that his future was even less clear.

The sales team leader, who has to evaluate the performance and give feedback based on the indicators, is more frustrated. Indeed, it is not easy to visit customers due to COVID-19, but the organization does not make decisions quickly—even if they want to change the indicators immediately. Although the sales team leader talked to the strategy team, they only emphasized the importance of objectification of control, management, and indicator measurement, saying that the salespeople should visit the customers through non-face-to-face sales activities, instead of complaining about the indicators. And the sales team leader thought there was nothing else left to do.

What would you do, if you were Kim's team leader? And how should we set and manage goals in the COVID era?[1]

With the changing environment due to COVID-19, should the sales departments be controlled and managed?

🚩 The issue that should be prioritized in the case above is to narrow the perspective difference between management and control of the sales team. The reason why the indicators cannot be readjusted when the customer visiting indicator is not realistic, is that the management of Company C views the sales department from a perspective of control. As working in the COVID era is changing to telecommuting and remote selling, indicators focusing on control and management are the first things to change.

However, Company C and many companies still doubt the sales department's working philosophy. In particular, as many companies have grown based on the manufacturing industry, Korean companies often regard sales teams as departments that cannot be managed and controlled. The following are interviews with company C's strategy team officials, and the sales team leader. We can see the concerns about setting indicators, distrust in each department, and perspective differences on control and management, due to COVID-19.

Q1. With the COVID-19 pandemic, are the existing performance indicators still meaningful?

Strategy Team Yes, we have many concerns, too. If COVID-19 is prolonged, I think we might need to change the performance indicators. However, though sales departments find it challenging to visit customers, sales have not significantly decreased. So I think salespeople will achieve better results if they try to visit customers more.

Q2. But it's indeed hard to visit customers these days, so shouldn't this situation be taken into account?

Strategy Team It is true that there are many complaints in the sales department. But even if it's not a face-to-face visit, phone calls or video sales are also possible. Still, I think we should include the performance indicator of visiting customers. Otherwise, it isn't easy to know what they're doing and whether they're meeting and managing customers properly.

Q3. Since the customer visit indicator was set last year, face-to-face sales has struggled prolongedly due to the worsening of COVID-19, so how should the performance indicator be improved?

Sales Team Leader Eventually, I think this is a matter of trust. The culture of sales departments is also changing. Young employees these days are especially reluctant to be controlled by such a regimented system. Now, I think salespeople should be able to try different things in an open-minded environment, like other development and marketing departments, and engage in sales activities autonomously. And we need to be able to discuss and revise goals regularly, according to the situation.

As the above conversation conveys, the company's strategy team and management show a distinct lack of trust in its own sales department. There are many reasons for that, but the biggest one is that the company's management thinks employees only work hard when they are managed and controlled. According to the interview, the company's management responded that they felt that the sales team was working properly only when it was under control, submitting reports daily. As a result, the sales team spent more time preparing these reports for internal evaluation instead of achieving its original sales goals, such as increasing sales revenue and customer satisfaction, which were naturally pushed back.

Which performance indicators are most suitable to the New Normal era?

After COVID-19, many organizations have been concerned about establishing measurement indicators. In the case of Company C mentioned above, the ultimate goal is to achieve the current year's sales targets and profits. However, when looking at the indicators in detail, we will find the 'customer visits' indicator included only at the organizational management level. The compensation also varies greatly depending on whether this indicator is achieved. Performance indicators should be tools to measure the sales activities and generate feedback to help achieve sales goals instead of tools only for organizational management. Moreover, we must consider how the indicators affect our goals in the COVID era. Since Company C is an equipment manufacturer, it is necessary to establish indicators that can measure sales more effectively than the number of customer visits.

Let's look at Company C's case again. In the case of Company C, only generic goals such as sales revenue, profits, and bond management were initially managed as KPIs. However, the CEO always complained that salespeople who have achieved their sales goals did not engage in sales activities, or make customer visits actively.

So, what came to mind was a performance indicator of the number of customer visits. However, Company C's policy not only caused complaints among their salespeople, but also delivered few results. Due to the policy of "visiting the customer four times per day," salespeople were faking the meaningless number of customer visits. During the process, they also lost opportunities to manage or sell to essential customers. Since the incorrect indicator (the number of customer visits) was included in the specific indicators to achieve the desired goals (sales revenue and profits), it brought entirely different results compared to what the organization intended to pursue. Therefore, organizations should try to reset measurement indicators to make them suitable for the post-COVID era, and diagnose whether our organization is going in the right direction.

Solution #1. Abandon your blind belief in measurement indicators

One of the most significant changes in the post-COVID era is digitalization. COVID-19 is rapidly changing the way each industry works. The way each sector performs also varies. In offline distribution, aviation, and travel industries, the gap between goals set earlier this year and the results is so large, that it is difficult even to measure performance. In this situation, it is necessary to consider whether the existing KPIs and performance management systems are meaningful. Perhaps we have a blind belief in measurement indicators as a scientific way of managing performance. Also, perhaps we are obsessed with performance indicators?

The blind belief in measurement is primarily influenced by American engineer Frederick Winslow Taylor, who coined the term "scientific management" as a way to increase industrial efficiency in the 1910s. To analyze the factory's iron production, Taylor subdivided the production process by component, determined the standard production level of each work to measure productivity, and applied different compensation plans to maximize productivity further. It was undoubtedly an effective method in a process that was measurable, and relatively simple to repeat.

The problem is that the obsession with these measurements is inconsistent with many organizations' direction, and does not keep up with the current changes. Company C, which we looked at earlier, is a typical example. Since they focused on performance measurement, only results that could be easily achieved were regarded as performance indicators, and evidence-based results were manipulated during practice. Many organizations often directly take the previous year's indicators, or mainly focus on the indicators that are easy to achieve when setting up KPIs at the end of the year. This is because instead of selecting indicators related to goals, indicators for evaluation and compensation are considered first.

The typical temptations of measuring indicators

1. Trying to measure the easiest thing.

2. Trying to to simplify the procedure, when complexity exists.

3. Trying to measure and decide the amount of input instead of the results, which affects the quality of the output.

4. Trying to focus on the standardization of the process, instead of understanding the situation and context for each case.

According to Campbell's Law," developed by U.S. social psychologist Donald Thomas Campbell, the more any quantitative social indicator is used for social decision-making, the more subject it will be to corruption pressures, and the more apt it will be to distort and corrupt the social processes it is intended to monitor. When dealing with measurement indicators, it is easy to fall into various temptations.[2] This is the reason why we should not only consider performance indicators and measurements in the post-COVID era.

For Company C, instead of focusing on the indicators for measurement, it is necessary to consider the sales goals and qualitative performance evaluation. Performance indicators can be a reference in heading toward the goals, but they should not be wholly trusted.

So far, we have looked at Company C's performance indicators, measurement methods, the nature of the chosen evaluation, and the reasons why they are unsuitable for the current situation. In the end, responding flexibly to the current situation should come first. As suggested in the previous interview, an autonomy-based working style should be adopted more often, instead of simply controlling and managing employees. In addition, instead of blindly concentrating on measurements, seeking changes and making adjustments through feedback, pivoting is necessary to achieve the organization's goals.

> **Pivoting** means giving up existing business projects and changing direction. Generally, it is regarded as an extreme measure, for when marketability is not as high as expected, or results are not produced. In this context, the term suggests that performance indicators must be flexibly modified according to the current situation.

Solution #2. Pivot performance indicators, based on how realistic they are

One problem with Company C's performance management is that it focuses on the action of visiting customers instead of achieving performance goals, which has been reflected in the unsuitable performance indicators in the COVID era. To reach the ultimate targets for the sales team, such as ensuring sales revenue, securing new customers, and selling new products, it is necessary to focus on realistic indicators to achieve performance goals. And when it is challenging to visit customers due to COVID-19, it is necessary to shift to realistic indicators suitable for the current situation.

If you focused on indicators for employee control and management before COVID-19, now you have to consider how much you have innovated your sales activities to cope with the current changes, and how these activities have affected your sales performance. In other words, to secure new customers, the production of marketing content and presentation materials, that can deliver messages more efficiently during online conferences or short meetings with customers, are regarded as more important. In addition, instead of focusing only on quantitative indicators when evaluating salespeople, performance management will be much more efficient when it includes the qualitative perspective, such as how efficiently salespeople engage in online sales like marketing activities. The qualitative view here refers to whether the marketing content produced is customer-friendly, and how much it can benefit the customers.

To focus on the qualitative performance of each salesperson, the organization should conduct the performance evaluation based on qualitative indicators that can boost the sales team's competencies, as well as offer corresponding coaching and communication according to the situation of the sales team, instead of evaluating them all

Company C's direction to improve performance indicators in the COVID era

AS-IS

Type	Content
Perfomance indicator	• Archievement of the sales revenue and profits • Number of visits for customer management
Mesurement point	• How many times and the how often is the customer visits realized to achieve sales results?

TO-BE

Type	Content
Perfomance indicator	• Adjustment of the sales revenue and profits * Factors to consider: industry average, the current competitor status • Qualitative evaluation of online sales activities • Online webinar customer status • Innovation in the way sales work, such as digital marketing and content production
Mesurement point	• How much has innovation in sales activities been carried out to respond to the change? • How did these activities affect business performance?

with the same quantitative indicators. As a result, to solve Company C's problem, performance indicators should not focus on measurement and control only. They should also be used as tools for goal setting (indicating the directions), task performing (standards of behavior), and diagnostic feedback (continuous communication during the task-performing process).

One of the mistakes many companies make is managing all sales teams' performance with the same criteria. Even for sales, the approaches to maximize their performance differ, depending on the region or the specific situation. It's like dressing different bodies in clothes of the same size, and viewing them from the same perspective. It is frustrating for salespeople to wear clothes that do not fit their bodies. In particular, these issues are bound to become more prominent because of the performance differences and changes, in each operational area and region, due to COVID-19.

Of course, managing performance with the same standards will lead to a common goal of increasing sales. But, suppose each sales team (considering regional and operational situations) is managed with specific, realistic indicators. In that case, the goals will be achieved more efficiently, and each sales team will also be able to act according to the current situation and the organization's strategy.

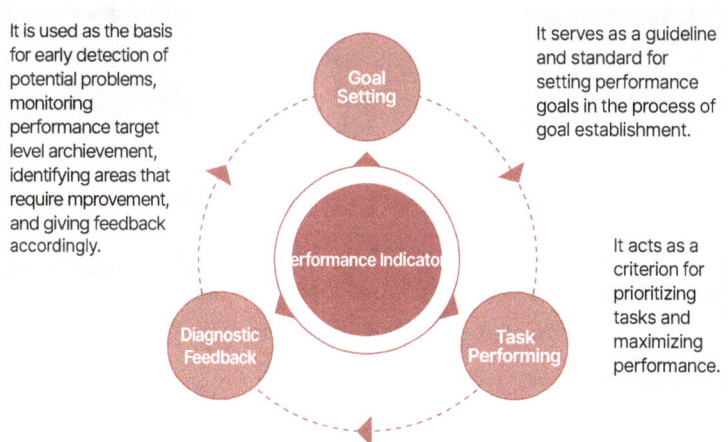

Roles and utilization of performance indicators

It is used as the basis for early detection of potential problems, monitoring performance target level archievement, identifying areas that require mprovement, and giving feedback accordingly.

It serves as a guideline and standard for setting performance goals in the process of goal establishment.

It acts as a criterion for prioritizing tasks and maximizing performance.

Goal Setting

Diagnostic Feedback

Task Performing

Performance Indicator

Solution #3. Change the evaluation and reward system

The traditional 'evaluation and reward' method can be said to have begun with the US military's 'merit system' during World War II. The merit system was used to judge, relocate, or retire underperformers. And after World War II, evaluation and compensation-oriented performance management were introduced to evaluate such underperformers, and used by more than 90% of the companies in the United States. The forced-ranking system, a relative evaluation system of GE that many companies benchmarked in the 1990s, is representative. GE emphasized responsibility for individual performance, and classified employees into A, B, and C grades. Grade A employees were compensated, and grade C employees were expelled.[3]

However, due to the impact of digital transformation and the increased complexity of the business environment, corporate evaluation and compensation systems are expected to shift significantly. A typical example is the abolition of relative evaluation systems, and the number of companies introducing the OKR[Objective and Key Results] system is increasing. Companies choose to make such changes because the limits of the previous system are becoming more apparent. A system that sets goals at the beginning of the year, and evaluates or rewards once a year or once every six months, has become something that no longer fits the realities of the COVID era.

> **OKR** A goal-setting framework that sets objectives and tracks results at the organizational level, using performance management techniques that were first initiated at Intel and expanded through Google to Silicon Valley.

However, many companies insist on maintaining the previous performance evaluation model, despite the flow of changes. Take Company C, for instance. Company C's performance management system focuses only on quantitative indicators for typical compensation. In addition, they focus only on oppressing and managing sales teams, with goals set once at the beginning of the year. The same goes for compensation. There are personal incentives, and individuals are compensated by being categorized into different grades, via the relative evaluation system. However, although individual competencies are critical in sales, the environment and various variables must also be considered. This is because the goals set at the beginning of the year may not fit the changing environment. Flexible responses are needed, depending on the region or the customer situation within the scope of responsibility. Therefore, for sales departments, rather than compensating individuals yearly, an approach that flexibly responds to the changing environment, such as quarterly goal setting and team-based compensation, is needed.

CASE STUDY

[Adobe] Check-in method and process

Adobe's Check-in is a relevant example. During cloud-based product sales, Adobe realized that the yearly evaluation method was too slow and time-consuming. They also found that the employees' ability to achieve their proposed KPIs at the beginning of the year depends on market conditions, but the existing system does not reflect them on time. To solve these problems, they introduced the Check-in system in 2013.

Adobe's Check-in system requires managers and team members to conduct quarterly performance review meetings at least once a quarter, and sometimes review meetings are held more often. Managers and team members can discuss and decide freely during the performance review meeting, instead of setting performance indicators in a fixed format. In other words, instead of being bound by form, communication focuses on the performance improvement of the work. In addition, unlike generic performance evaluations, it is also characterized by not assigning grades or scores.

Adobe has made several positive changes and achievements since the introduction of Check-in. The most significant difference is that the negative features of the existing performance evaluation system have improved. The existing performance evaluation inevitably had a negative vibe, which emphasized the deficiencies to help assess and decide the corresponding compensation once a year. Yet the Check-in system made it possible to have lively conversations in a positive atmosphere, conducive to individual performance improvement and development. Depending on the situation, the goals were checked from time to time, making it possible to respond quickly. The resignation rate decreased by 30%, and leaders saved 80,000 hours of performance evaluation reports writing.[4]

During the post-COVID era, instead of staying with the existing, standardized performance measurement method, it is necessary to respond with flexibility and make changes by focusing on improving future competencies. At this time, it is imperative to share opinions on the things that were done well in the past, where weaknesses could be found, and what should be improved. It is also more important to consider how to apply the improvement points from the current situation to future strategies. That's why the leaders' role as coaches has become more critical in the post-COVID era.

> **Check-in process**
>
> 1. At the beginning of the year, expectations are set between managers and team members through meetings.
>   * However, the expected goals can be reviewed and adjusted periodically.
>
> 2. Feedback meetings between managers and team members should be held at least once a quarter. Feedback should be provided to focus on performance and improve competencies and outcomes by conducting it frequently whenever necessary in addition to the regular meetings.
>
> 3. There is no set framework or format when setting goals or delivering feedback, and formal procedures such as review reports, as in the past, should be avoided.
>
> 4. There are no rankings or scores for relative evaluation.

Simply evaluating and compensating is something anyone can do. Now, we need a partner role who contemplates issues or difficulties with the sales team, and helps suggest directions.

Differences between the existing performance evaluation method and the Check-in system

Type	Annual performance review	Check-in system
Goal setting	• Set up at the beginning of the year and proceed without modifications	• Set expected goals, regularly discuss with the managers, and make revisions and improvements along the way
Feedback	• Time-consuming, the evidence and results for performance evaluation are written separately, and the procedure of giving feedback is carried out once (negative experience)	• Formal document preparation is unnecessary, and continuous conversation between leaders and team members is the key
Evaluation and compensation	• To determine annual salary and incentives, a complicated rating and ranking process is required	• There is no formal evaluation, ranking, or rating process • Annual salary is based on performance (absolute evaluation) * Decisions are made with not exceeding the overall budget
Feedback cycle	• The period of giving feedback is set once or twice a year under the supervision of the HR team, and most feedback-giving sessions are formal and aimed at deciding year-end compensation and bonus	• It is conducted at least once a quarter and is continuously carried out by focusing on improving productivity and fostering competencies for the team
Education	• Manager coaching courses are provided by the HR department (regular courses)	• In addition to training, real-time support for coaching managers and Q&A are also provided * face-to-face, non-face-to-face

Source: https://www.adobe.com/check-in.html

Points of "performance management" sales leaders should think of in the New Normal era

⚑ Earlier, we looked at how sales departments should manage performance indicators in the post-COVID era. From now on, we will discuss leadership-related points to be considered by sales leaders, in the post-COVID period.

Should you control them? Or give them autonomy?

> "We don't know what the sales team is doing. They won't even fill out the sales records properly if we don't check them. So, our company designates the daily number of customer visits, and monitors and controls them daily. Our company's new business sales are low because the sales team is not actively selling. I will discuss this with the sales leaders who are in charge."

This is an excerpt from an actual interview with a company's management. After monitoring the company's sales team for a few days, it felt like the top priority of the sales team was to be less criticized by the management. Salespeople were repeating meaningless sales activities, such as dropping down senseless sales records, or visiting unnecessary customers (customer cold calling or video meetings after the outbreak of COVID-19). From the customer's point of view, it was impossible to be content to have an arrangement with a salesperson without obtaining anything. Instead, there were cases where these sales activities had adverse effects, harming the brand. What was more serious was the perceptions and attitudes of the employees. When a problem was identified during monitoring, the question "Why don't you take action?" was met with the following response: "Well, I originally suggested an improvement plan for the problems you mentioned. But they told me that it's not my job, and that I should only focus on meeting customers." In the end, most salespeople were not focusing on achieving the company's goals, but were thinking of changing jobs or killing time by filling the daily required number of customer visits.

Aren't many sales departments already accustomed to a toxic culture that lacks trust and belief like this? In the past, leaders' fundamental perception was based on 'Theory X,' which means they did not trust their members, and viewed them as objects to control. According to Theory X, humans hate to work and are only motivated by economic benefits. Therefore, they thought their employees were unreliable, and could be driven only by strict supervision, control, management, and financial compensation. On the other hand, 'Theory Y' posits that, for employees, working is not just about economic compensation, but also about fully expressing one's abilities and achieving one's self-realization. According to Theory Y, managers should provide employees with conditions to work autonomously and creatively.[5]

In the past, performance management focused on controlling and managing may have been possible. This is because the results could be achieved by monitoring what was wrong within the system and then applying a standardized way of work. This control system was more challenging to give up, because it gave the management a sense of belief and satisfaction that the company was running as it should. It also set the management's mind at ease when it came to managing and monitoring. In other words, giving responsibility and autonomy to the sales team was difficult, because the leadership believed that a standardized system was more efficient and could maximize performance. However, in the current COVID era, it is almost impossible to assume that the leadership can control and manage everything. To respond appropriately to the working environment of remote selling, the ever-changing market environment, and customer needs, it is more efficient to trust employees and delegate tasks properly. Therefore, instead of controlling and managing, the leadership should determine if the current sales strategy and direction fit the company's goals, and offer recommendations for further development through periodic meetings with the sales team.

The management of a company that does not trust their sales team thinks that their selected employees are lacking in abilities or are unreliable, based on the presupposition that their employees are not working correctly. This presupposition is wrong. If the management has chosen an excellent sales team, they should create an environment to ensure the sales performance can be maximized. Although the management claimed that they had given the sales team authority to conduct work, the sales team can never take the lead if the number of daily customer visits is checked and micromanagement is implemented to see whether the salespeople are working correctly. Moreover, we experienced drastic changes first hand throughout the year 2020. In order to actively respond to such a rapidly changing business environment and uncertainties, it is necessary to create a self-directing work environment, in which members can take operational initiatives based on trust instead of control and management. The word 'self-directed' here should not be misunderstood. Granting autonomy does not mean that there are no rules. It means having freedom within the organization's regulations and framework.

The power of trust and autonomy is more substantial than we think. I want to introduce an experiment on how the power of trust affects performance. In one experiment, the researchers randomly selected one employee, praised this employee as excellent, and raised their performance goals. After 3 to 12 months, the honored employees became excellent employees. In a study of U.S. Navy officer candidates and employees working in the heavy industry, 12-17% of employees achieved 'excellent' status at work due to the Pygmalion effect. In this way, employees can achieve better results if they have goals, a sense of mission, and receive complete trust from their organizations.[6]

Now, let's look at the results of a study on the power of autonomy. A truck company experimented by dividing the managers into two groups. One group allowed employees to autonomously decide and choose the service coverage and how to handle customer complaints. In contrast, the other group only allowed managers to make all the decisions, and the employees could only follow instructions. What was the result? Four months later, the autonomous group reported that organizational commitment and job satisfaction increased, while the frequency of accidents decreased.[7]

Organizations based on trust and autonomy create a positive and forward-looking environment of "Let's give it a try." If salespeople are immersed in such an environment, continuous challenges, innovations, and work improvements will occur more actively. Companies that seek innovation through coercion, control, and management cannot achieve success and innovation in its true sense. As a result of Harvard Business School's analysis of innovative companies, all companies that continuously innovate were based on a culture of autonomy.[8] There may still be leaders who think it is not easy to deliver sales results unless everything is controlled and managed. However, to survive in the COVID era, innovation is essential. This is why leaders should deviate from the perspective of control and management.

Are you a Theory X believer, or are you leading your team based on Theory Y? Leaders reading this, should consider what kind of thought process they use to lead their teams. It is recommended to consider the prerequisites, in order to successfully lead sales teams in the post-COVID era.

Extrinsic motivation vs. Intrinsic motivation

Many companies are experiencing difficulties in managing their performance. In particular, issues arise in evaluation and compensation. Recently, there have been cases in which members are protesting about compensation issues in several large companies, which is eventually an issue of how to view and deal with performance management and indicators. The problem is that almost all companies use the performance quantified through these indicators only as a tool to differentiate their members' compensation. However, suppose a member is evaluated only by such figures, which later decide their compensation. In that case, even if the results are wrong and have no relation to actual management performance, everyone might still be pursuing similar goals, which can be a side effect of this procedure. This should not be a proper motivation. In practice, members do not simply seek financial incentives.

What direction, then, should we pursue in performance management during the post-COVID era? Standardizing the performance evaluation procedure in the post-COVID era is difficult. This is because as the environment changes, the way people work shifts accordingly. Instead of simply quantifying the work through performance indicators like before, disconnecting the compensation and evaluations is more efficient. Therefore, it is necessary to focus on intrinsic motivation such as growth, improvement, culture, and autonomy, instead of extrinsic financial motivation. This is because organizational members can be motivated by feedback for development and improvement, instead of financial incentives to diagnose the future direction and move forward. In addition, since it has become difficult for leaders to manage their members in detail like before during situations like telecommuting, it has become more important to instill intrinsic motivation in organizational members' minds, to empower them to move forward on their own.

Some might think, "Outcome numbers are vital for sales departments. So, I disagree that intrinsic motivation is more important than extrinsic motivation." However, you will probably change your mind if you encounter the following situation.

Salesman A is a star performer, recognized by everyone in the company. However, after COVID-19, A's performance indicators have bottomed out. It has also become challenging to achieve good results in the performance appraisal. This is because business performance plummeted, due to the prolonged pandemic in the region where A was in charge. A was frustrated by being classified as an underperformer even though A worked hard, following the company's policies and guidelines. Moreover, as performance fell, A became the company's scapegoat when it came to control and management, and A's subsequent loss of motivation worsened things. A's team leader wants to motivate A, but cannot develop any good ideas. It has become challenging to encourage A, because the company offers feedback and rewards based on performance indicators.

Motivating A would not be easy, even if you were A's team leader. The problem is not simply about receiving less compensation. Motivating employees through standardizing the performance indicators and utilizing the extrinsic financial reward is embedded in the company's system and policies. From the team leader's point of view, A may at least be a little motivated and inspired by being offered performance recognition and work autonomy, even if the financial reward is small. However, this can be realized only if the company's policy or system changes. Moreover, even though COVID-19 is a constantly changing factor, if management and feedback-giving are based on the performance evaluation, standardized via the same set of indicators used in the past, it is not only difficult for A to find the intrinsic motivation for growth and achievement but also likely to give A a sense of skepticism.

Paying attention to the organizational members' thoughts on extrinsic and intrinsic motivation, it becomes clearer why we should focus on intrinsic instead of extrinsic motivation. The following are some results of the organizational diagnosis of 349 Company H's service department employees. One interesting thing pops up when looking at the survey results. The organization's leaders thought that the motivational factors that their employees considered necessary were a sense of belonging, financial compensation, and welfare benefits (about 20%). However, most employees answered that problem solving (growth and successful experiences) and positive feedback from customers (about 94%) were more important than money or welfare. Only 3% of employees said financial compensation and a sense of belonging were more criti-

The survey results from the employees

Q. What makes you feel most rewarding(satisfied) while working?

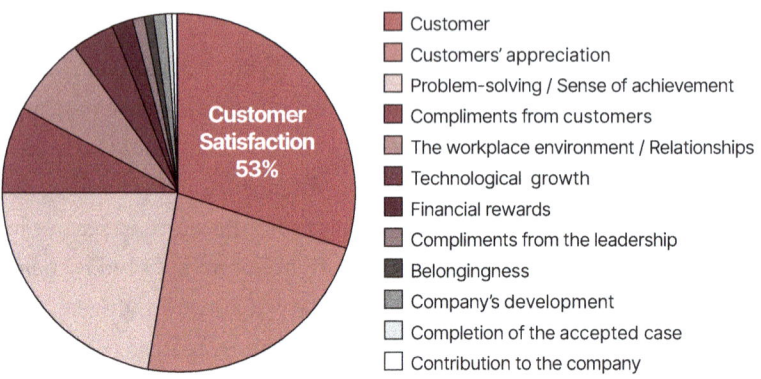

Type	Respondent	Percentage
Customer satisfaction	105	30%
Customers' appreciation	80	23%
Problem-solving/Sense of achievement	78	22%
Compliments from customers	28	8%
The workplace environment / Relationships	24	7%
Technological growth	15	4%
Financial rewards	8	2%
Compliments from the leadership	5	1%
Belongingness	2	1%
Company's development	2	1%
Total	349	

Source: Survey Results of Company H's Service Department (2020)

cal. The survey results may not represent all organizations, but one thing that can be certain is hat employees do not only pursue extrinsic motivations.

The importance of intrinsic motivation is more evident in an experiment conducted in 1971 by Professor Edward L. Deci, at the University of Rochester.

He experimented, assuming that if an employee whose performance was driven by intrinsic motivation (one's interests and enthusiasm) received extrinsic rewards (money or other compensation), the performance would drop. The experiment was conducted by dividing participants into two groups, and having them put together a Soma puzzle. During the experiment, participants were asked to reproduce various paintings drawn on paper, using puzzle pieces. And in the space where the assignment was performed, reading materials like The New Yorker, Time, and Playboy were provided, to prevent them from focusing on puzzle-building. The researchers measured the puzzle completion time after assigning participants the task. The experiment lasted three days. On day one, both groups were asked to solve puzzle quizzes. On day two, for each puzzle completed within a limited time, one group was offered a dollar, and the other group was offered nothing. On day three, the last day, neither group was rewarded.

During the experiment, the researchers gave participants eight minutes of free time. The difference between the two groups was revealed during this time. The group which had never been rewarded played freely with puzzles even during their free time, but the group that received money on the second day showed different results before and after the reward. On day two, when compensation was given, 67.7 seconds were used to solve the puzzles during free time. Yet, on the third day, when the rewards stopped, their interest was significantly reduced, and the gap with the uncompensated control group widened.[9]

This experiment confirmed that changing someone's behavior, or producing results with extrinsic or tangible rewards, can adversely affect motivation. Professor Edward L. Deci and professor Richard Ryan indicated that three needs must be met to continue providing intrinsic motivation. The three needs are competence, autonomy, and relatedness. First, competence is the desire to exercise one's ability and to be competent. This is related to a sense of achievement. When faced with challenges or complex tasks, growing daily with the proper feedback, we will be able to improve our competencies and increase our level of achievement.

Second, autonomy refers to the desire for self-control in performing tasks. In the previous case of Company C, it was confirmed that the bureaucratic and vertical organizational structure hindered autonomy and motivation.

Finally, relatedness means feeling connected to others, and realizing a sense of belonging. When you feel comfortable and connected to your colleagues, you can safely share your opinions and emotions, and you will be intrinsically motivated. In the COVID era, it became tough to find that sense of belonging, due to the increase in telecommuting. Thus, leaders should consider how to make their employees feel that, and how to make them feel connected to each other. In other words, making it possible for organizational members to satisfy their relationship-oriented desire has become an essential issue for leaders.[10]

Though we have heard countless times about the importance of intrinsic motivation, we need to consider it further in the post-COVID era. Intrinsic motivation is the core issue related to performance management, motivation mechanism, evaluation, and compensation of sales departments we have looked at in this chapter. Leaders should think harder about their sales goals in this changing environment, as well as about the management philosophy they will adopt.

Top-down goal-setting vs. Bottom-up goal-setting

Many companies make great efforts to set goals every October. In particular, sales departments sometimes work overnight while establishing goals and strategies. Companies are obsessed with this process, because they want to maximize performance by aligning the company's goals with each department's and employee's goals. Secondly, it is also for the sake of efficiency within management. As seen in the examples we explored earlier, it is relatively efficient for managers to set specific numbers to control their employees. The last reason is compensation. Like GE's Rank and Yank system, which is a performance-based system, it intends to compensate people by ranking them from first to last, and filter out those who rank too low.

> **Rank and Yank** is the process by which a company ranks employees by comparing them to each other, while expelling the employees with the lowest ranking through a low-performers program.[11]

However, everyone with experience in the workplace may have made mistakes in goal setting and performance management. Regardless of this year's performance, some get better evaluated because it's time for them to be promoted, or because someone had a poor performance appraisal last year. Moreover, the organizational leaderships often appoint goals for each department or employee from a top-down approach. In reality, Korean companies face the problem that, even if they established goals and strategies overnight based on collected data and market growth and reported them to the team leader or to higher leadership, the employees of each department would still have to follow the plans from the top down. Nevertheless, goals set from the top down for sales teams are even more meaningless.

Recently, I visited a shop to purchase an air purifier. I looked around for a long time, and a salesperson approached and explained the product in detail. When I was about to make my purchase, the salesperson said, "Would it be okay for you to make this purchase three days later? I can get you more freebies by that time." I did not need the air purifier urgently, and waiting two to three days didn't make a big difference, so I said yes and asked the salesperson, "Did you achieve your sales goal for this month?" It turned out that the salesperson had asked me to come back later so that I could help them achieve next month's performance target—since this month's sales goal was already accomplished.

Perhaps the leaders reading this book have similar experiences, or have seen their team members doing the same thing. This is why companies should reconsider their one-sided assigned goals.

In the post-COVID era, one-sided target assignment is becoming less relevant. Due to the increase in telecommuting, working autonomy is naturally strengthened. As a result, it becomes challenging for team leaders to manage and supervise employees who work in a place they cannot see. In this era, the one-sided assigned goals or performance targets no longer work.

The method of goal-setting should also be reconsidered. The basic goal-setting process is as follows: first, the company's performance over the past two to three years needs to be analyzed. In addition, the performance of the next three years should be predicted, considering the market growth rate. However, at this point, completely different results may be derived, depending on how the scope is set. For example, suppose that growth was slow due to industrial underdevelopment until three years ago, but last year's launch of a new product led to a sharp increase in growth. Then, should we adopt the average growth rate over the past five years? Or should we set higher developmental goals to reflect last year's growth rate? Of course, from the management's point of view, we should choose the latter. Then, can we say that we made the right predictions and set reasonable goals?

In one experiment, participants were given a short article, describing an intern teacher's class. Among the participants, Group A was asked to evaluate the quality of the class (in percentiles) based on the article, and Group B was asked to assess the standing of this intern teacher in five years, based on the same piece. As a result, the scores given by the two groups were the same. In other words, there is no significant difference between evaluating the information (quality of the class) on which the prediction is based, or predicting the future (whether or not the intern teacher will succeed in 5 years). It is a very extreme example, but it is not much different from predicting future performance based on past performance. Eventually, we predict the future with only a little information. This is because we have no choice but to consider only the fragmentary issues instead of the overall context, such as not considering the changing environment, and setting goals based on existing achievements.[12]

Performance evaluation and prediction can be extreme, and projections are bound to be inaccurate. Moreover, no matter how precise predictions are, it is easy to lose direction in situations when we do not know when COVID-19 will end, or how the consumption trend will change. COVID-19 may suddenly appear in the area I am in charge of, and my current goals may become meaningless. Now that the future is unpredictable, we must reconsider the goals that we have set so far. As discussed earlier, it is time to seriously consider realistic goal setting that the employees agree with, instead of one-sided goal setting or prediction, based on only one incident or leader.

Mechanical approach vs. pursuing diversity

We have only emphasized efficient management, manuals, and mechanized processes through performance indicators. Thus, strategies and policies were established by the company's leadership or strategy department, and the employees achieved specific results by following these policies. The reason companies try to control organizational members with performance indicators alone, may be due the so-called 'temptation of the scientific performance management,' or the legacy of the past where performance can be maximized by following the management's doctrine mechanically. This mechanical approach may be more efficient in a predictable business environment, or a workplace where results can be delivered by simple work. But will it be the same in a VUCA environment as the ones created during the COVID era? Probably not.

> **VUCA** Abbreviation for Volatility, Uncertainty, Complexity, and Ambiguity. It refers to an unsteady social environment. It was first used at the US Army War College, in the early 1990s.[13]

Mechanical approaches have side effects, such as lowering creativity and the depth of thinking. A series of experiments conducted by Abraham Samuel Luchins, a professor and psychologist at the State University of New York, clearly demonstrates the influence of this mechanical approach. Luchins experimented with a water jar problem. Three jars were used in the experiment: jar A could hold 21 cups of water, jar B 127 cups, and jar C 3 cups. The goal was to fill one of these three jars with a fixed amount of water. Luchins asked the participants how they would go about adding precisely 100 cups of water in one jar.

The answer was as follows: first, fill jar B with water, then fill jar A with the water from jar B. Jar B now contains 106 cups of water. Next, fill jar C with the water from jar B. Discard the water in jar C, and repeat this process once more. Then, 100 cups of water are left in jar B. During the experiment, six of these kinds of questions were presented. Participants who solved the problem a few times, found a formula they applied to all problems. The procedure was to fill jar A with the water from jar B, and then fill jar C with the water from jar B twice. Participants solved the problem by applying the same rule to all of the problems.

However, Luchins presented another five questions, changing the problem's setup without giving any hints to the participants. Suppose jar A can hold 14 cups of water, jar B 36 cups of water, and jar C 8 cups of water. What should you do to fill a jar with precisely 6 cups of water? Of course, the previous formula can also be applied to this problem. Fill jar A with the water from jar B, leaving 22 cups of water in jar B. After that, fill jar C with the water from jar B twice, leaving exactly six cups of water in jar B. But there is a more straightforward solution. If you fill jar A with water and pour that water in jar C, then only 6 cups of water will remain in jar A. Nevertheless, 83% of the participants applied the previously existing procedure. The control group skipped the previous experiment, was immediately asked the questions from the second round, and 80% of the participants were able to give a more straightforward solution.[14]

Hence, we have a bad habit of continuing to use the same procedure when we get used to it. This bad habit does not fit the post-

COVID era, which requires a quick change of stance. In other words, it is time to reconsider whether we can solve the problem with a mechanical approach, in the ever-changing COVID era. In the age of VUCA, thinking more flexibly should be pursued.

The case of performance indicators discussed earlier is a typical case of a mechanical approach and process. Now it's time to listen to the voices of the employees working in the field, and apply new and diverse methods instead.

CHECKLIST

Post-COVID era, sales leader's performance management diagnosis table

Category	Checklist
Performance indicators	☐ Are indicators set to suit the changing environment (non-face-to-face sales business environment)?
	☐ Aren't you evaluating 'just for the sake of evaluating,' only focusing on standardization and compensation?
	☐ Are the indicators connected (aligned) with the company's goals? Aren't you compensating with the wrong indicators?
	☐ Aren't you having a blind belief toward the measurement indicators?
Performance management	☐ Aren't you assigning one-sided performance targets from the top down?
	☐ Aren't you conducting formal performance management and feedback-giving yearly?
	☐ Are you focusing on periodic feedback, growth, and improvement?
Changes in the way you work	☐ Aren't you leading the team with a focus on control and management?
	☐ Is the department operated under the consideration of intrinsic motivational factors such as autonomy, competence, and relatedness?
	☐ Do you adopt a mechanical approach? Or do you pursue diversity?

Chapter 4

Sales New Normal #4
Changes in fostering and coaching

What are the sales leaders' roles and necessary competencies in the New Normal era?

The prolonged COVID-19 has created another task for sales leaders: how to coach and give feedback to team members, in a non-face-to-face environment that is entirely different from the past. Even if the external environment changes, the core of coaching does not change. The key to coaching is to show how to achieve better results. However, there are certain areas where leadership needs to change in response to the changing environment. Instead of acting based on existing approaches or stereotypes, and assumptions related to existing businesses, it is time to establish a new perspective and break free from those assumptions.

Previously, we have looked at how sales departments work, and sales leaders' goal-setting and performance management approaches in the post-COVID era. Now, let's look at the competencies that sales leaders should have, and how to lead the sales team members in the post-COVID era.

CASE STORY 3

New Normal era,
'Leader's thoughts vs. Members' thoughts'

* The story is based on a true story, and some details/information have been changed.

Team leader K, a sales team leader at a health food manufacturing company, has been delivering extraordinary results ever since he was a simple salesperson. In particular, based on the bulldozer-like sales propulsion and relationship-oriented sales approaches, K's outstanding performance has been on a roll regardless of domestic or overseas sales. He, who has led the domestic sales team, has been busy every day since the outbreak of COVID-19 in 2019, as he has been appointed to manage part of the overseas sales department. As with any sales team, the problem is the sales performance. Performance is of vital importance since 'outcome numbers' are regarded as critical for sales teams. However, it has not been easy to deliver results due to the influence of COVID-19. K was also exhausted, to the point where he started drinking due to stress, which he did not often do. In particular, as overseas exports declined due to COVID, the team's sales performance worsened, and K lost ground following the trend. To make things worse, K was worried and anxious since the salespeople seemed to be less effective after they were encouraged by the company to work from home. If he could, he would like to step up and directly engage in sales, as he did when he was a salesperson. Yet, it is difficult for him to participate in everything personally, and many uncertainties are involved in the changing business environment due to COVID-19. He has solved many problems through a charismatic leadership and sales style, but he feels that communication with employees has been ineffective in this telecommuting environment.

When did the problems first start to show? The following is a video meeting conversation conducted by team leader K, who promised to encourage and lead the team members to explore new markets, with assistant managers D and J in charge of the overseas sales.

Team Leader K D, I have received the report on the online video conference that was submitted yesterday. Was there anything special?
Assistant Manager D No, there weren't any significant problems.
Team Leader K The report indicated that some buyers showed interest, was there any potential buyer that would lead to sales results?
Assistant Manager D The Spanish buyer asked a few questions. Since it was a conference where all the buyers were gathered, and we didn't know their quarantine policies and conditions, the response was a little insufficient.
Team Leader K Didn't you prepare your answers beforehand? What was J doing? You guys attended the conference together, didn't you? If someone was interested, you should have offered them individual consultation services! Why didn't you push harder?
Assistant Manager J Um… Since we're not used to video consultation sessions yet, inviting the Spanish buyer to a separate meeting was something that didn't come up naturally…
Team Leader K Did you schedule a time for a follow-up meeting?
Assistant Manager D Not yet…
Team Leader K D! How on earth are you handling your work? You're not fully prepared before the meeting and don't follow up after the session! Can't you see our team's sales status quo this year? You two have the lowest goal achievement rate; what are you even thinking when conducting sales?
Assistant Manager D & J …

Team Leader K Are you sure you are working from home properly? Every time you talk about the proposal, you say you're still preparing it. From now on, write down what kind of work you did each day, and submit it with a report file attached. It's so frustrating.
Assistant Manager D & J Okay. I will.

After the video conference
Assistant Manager D I really can't take this. J, what's wrong with the team leader?
Assistant Manager J I guess there's a lot of performance pressure from top management these days. He was a candidate for the executive position, but after the team expanded, the sales performance was not as expected.
Assistant Manager D Does he think it's easy to work in such a changing environment? I mean, if we're not doing an excellent job, maybe he should stop lecturing and offer us some help... I'm going crazy.
Assistant Manager J It's better to do it independently, and then report. If the team leader comes to the meeting, it only means more work. He's not good at handling online meeting tools, which will cause more trouble.
Assistant Manager D Well, that's very true. At least it was a video conference; otherwise, there could have been more problems. J, you're definitely having a hard time. Are you coming to the office next week?
Assistant Manager J Yes, I'm coming for two days. I'll see you then.
Assistant Manager D All right. Let's figure out what the team leader told us to do.

In the above example, it can be said that the issues K experienced were not a big deal before the COVID era. Before COVID-19, sales team leaders received face-to-face reports from their members every day and, if necessary, they also went to customer meetings with the sales team members. More detailed things could be checked and taken care of when conducting face-to-face sales. It was not that difficult for the sales team leader K to lead and coach his team, because he had rich experiences in offline-based sales activities. Plus, it was the team leader's responsibility to manage the team.

What is your organization like? After COVID-19, we must check whether these things are happening in our company's sales department. Many organizational leaders have experienced operational difficulties due to changes in the company's work style and customer needs. Therefore, after COVID-19, the leaders' role and ability to perform the corresponding responsibilities should change.

Changes in the role of sales leaders: autocratic leadership no longer works

As mentioned earlier, COVID-19 has brought about a significant change in the way many sales departments operate. Customers are reluctant toward salespeople's visits, and as companies switch to telecommuting, sales are often performed online instead of face-to-face. In addition, online meetings are usually conducted using rapidly growing online meeting platforms such as Zoom, Microsoft Teams, and Webex. Conferences are now being held online using platforms such as YouTube Live instead of large venues like hotel banquet halls.

In this environment, what roles should the sales team leaders play to drive their sales team to achieve results?

In the post-COVID era, sales leaders should escape from the past's autocratic and authoritarian leadership styles, and shift to lead the team and their members based on a horizontal organizational structure. It's similar to the role of a coach in sports games. Leaders reading this may think, haven't we talked about this before? Of course, there have been many discussions around this kind of leadership. But the important thing here is that the environment has changed completely.

When COVID-19 was in full swing, a friend from a financial company's HR team contacted me. The friend tried to ask for advice, saying many issues arose because of the rapidly changing environment. According to the friend, the financial company was trying to speed up decision-making and create a horizontal organizational culture by dividing the organization, which consisted of large teams in the past, into smaller units. The leaders were often confused because of the organizational structure and how they work, which had changed significantly compared to the past. Before COVID-19, the company required leaders to manage the organization with the appropriate instructions and commands. However, in the rapidly changing COVID era, effective communication and horizontal coordination of opinion exchanges among members should be enabled even in a non-face-to-face environment, and faster decision-making is required within the organization. Indeed, this kind of change has already been attempted with the spread of agile management culture, even before COVID-19. Then, as COVID-19 accelerated, rapid organizational changes took place.

As can be seen from the table, in the past, it was common to operate sales departments in an authoritarian way, with an emphasis on standardization. However, in the COVID era, horizontal communication with organizational members has become more critical with the changes in working, corporate culture, and a hyper-

Changes in sales leadership before and after COVID-19

Type	Before COVID-19 Management based on vertical organizational culture (Taylorism)	After COVID-19 Management based on horizontal organizational culture (Agile Management)
Leadership Style	• Command and control • Autocratic/bureaucratic leadership	• Value autonomy, responsibility, and intrinsic motivation. • Emphasize horizontal organizational structure and adaptability to change • A coaching type of leadership
Management method	• Seek efficiency through measurement • Focus on standardization	• Respect individual characteristics • Communication is based on a horizontal culture • Aim to create sales departments that can quickly respond to the market with an agile organizational structure and management Sales approach
Sales approach	• Offline face-to-face sales • Seek seller/manufacturer-centric efficiency	• Online, non-face-to-face sales • On/Off hybrid sales approaches • Customer-centered approach to suit the hyper-personalized environment

personalized environment where each individual's characteristics are respected. At the financial company mentioned earlier, the existing vertical and bureaucratic approach no longer works, as companies now must pursue an agile organizational structure (simplifying the organization's structure to respond quickly to various issues). Somehow, it might seem natural. Although the market is rapidly changing, if organizational members are in an authoritative environment where they have to follow the team leader's instructions and orders, it makes the horizontal coordination of opinion exchanges and responses based on actual sales experiences difficult. The team may also miss the timing for development, and fall behind competitors.

The hyper-personalization issue has become a hot topic ever since two to three years ago. Hyper-personalization refers to providing products or services by predicting customers' preferences (needs), after identifying the consumer contextual situations in real-time. This era of hyper-personalization accelerated with the outbreak of COVID-19. With the advent of the contact-free age, the big data accumulated so far began to be connected to non-face-to-face technology. Companies that provide hyper-personalized services by precisely reading customers' thoughts, minds, and behavioral data are leading the post-COVID market.[1]

This hyper-personalization phenomenon is also emphasized in organizational operations and sales. Considering the characteristics of each corporate member, different communication approaches and coaching styles should be applied. This means that a more detailed approach is required. The standardized communication approach of the past no longer works. That's why changing the leaders' role from vertical leadership to coaching is essential. The era of sitting still and giving instructions and orders is over. As leaders, you should be able to respond quickly to the changing market, such as putting yourself in your team members' shoes, and promptly picking up and applying new methodologies during contact-free sales.

Sales leaders' coaching method: change the theme and style

As can be seen in the cases of Audi, Hyundai Motor Company, and team leader K's sales experience discussed earlier in the book, salespeople's digital competency is becoming increasingly critical. Accordingly, sales leaders' coaching themes and styles should also change. If conversation skills with customers and knowledge of products were the previous main themes in coaching, now the crucial issues will be what preparations are needed in advance to effectively discover and communicate with customers in a non-face-to-face environment, what tools to use, and how to communicate effectively in such an environment. Of course, this doesn't mean that communication skills or product knowledge is insignificant. Sales leaders in the New Normal era need to think about how this knowledge and skills can be applied in a changing environment, and try to find better solutions with their salespeople.

The coaching style of one-sided leadership should also change. Who in the team makes the best use of tools such as YouTube, Zoom, and Microsoft Teams, which are recently used for video conferences and online meetings with customers? Of course, the answer may be the sales leader, who is always equipped with new technologies, but most of the time, the younger MZ generation members may be more familiar with how to use these tools. Therefore, it is efficient to conduct tool-based and content-based coaching separately.

It will be possible to strengthen the competencies of the sales department more effectively and efficiently if the team coaching is dualized, receiving help from junior team members in terms of tool utilization, and valuing experienced leaders' opinions for content-based coaching. Coaching is not only realized by leaders, but by the best person in each field, which will be beneficial to the entire team. In particular, if previously coaching was done in the form of closed learning led by leaders, and conducted based on experience, now it should be in the form of open learning; that is, everyone should lead learning and share experiences within the team.

It is the first time anyone has conducted sales in the post-COVID era. Not even the sales team leader has a perfect solution for this age. Of course, experiences may lead to better strategy-making. However, what the leader says is not always the answer. Leaders need the willingness to respond flexibly and open-mindedly to their environment. To make this possible, there must be an organizational culture in which members can freely share ideas and grow together. This should be based on a growth mindset, which is the belief that individuals can continue to grow through challenges and failures.

Changes in the leaders' coaching before and after COVID-19

Type	Before COVID-19	After COVID-19
Coaching theme	• Communication skills with customers • Product knowledge • Overall sales process	• Sales direction in a non-face-to-face environment • Non-face-to-face sales communication/tool utilization
Coaching style	• Accompanying sales when visiting customers • Offline-based face-to-face coaching/feedback	• After non-face-to-face video sales (when the leader attends) • Non-face-to-face basis, respecting individual characteristics • Emphasizing communication based on a horizontal culture
Coaching subject/ approach	• Sales leader • Closed learning (based on leaders' experiences)	• Delegating responsibilities and fostering learning based on members' specialty • Open learning (member-led learning) • Pursuing a sales department that can respond quickly to the market with an agile structure and operations

If a leader leads the organization with a fixed mindset that "no matter how hard someone tries, his/her intelligence and talents will not change," they will fail to respond to the rapidly changing environment quickly, and won't be able to thrive during the COVID era. The first step to an agile organization is to allow failure, and react promptly to the market.[2]

Sales leaders' competence development: keep up with the times

Most organizations have made great efforts to develop competencies in the sales sector, in order to drive performance. In particular, various methods were attempted to strengthen the competencies of sales leaders, who exert the most significant influence in sales departments. At critical times, such as when new competitors and products emerge or new products are launched, the organization has no choice but to focus on developing sales leaders' competencies, since sales leaders' abilities could significantly influence the organization's performance. The problem is that COVID-19 inevitably changed the competencies of sales leaders. New, necessary competencies have appeared, and organizations have also changed their priorities of various previously required competencies for sales leaders. So, what competencies are required of sales leaders in the COVID era?

According to a survey on the perceptions of leaders inside an organization, conducted by the research institute Embrain in July 2020, organizational members felt that the leaders' competency was more critical after COVID-19. And differences in leadership were more apparent.

62% of the respondents answered that, after COVID-19, the role of leaders in departments/teams seemed to have become more

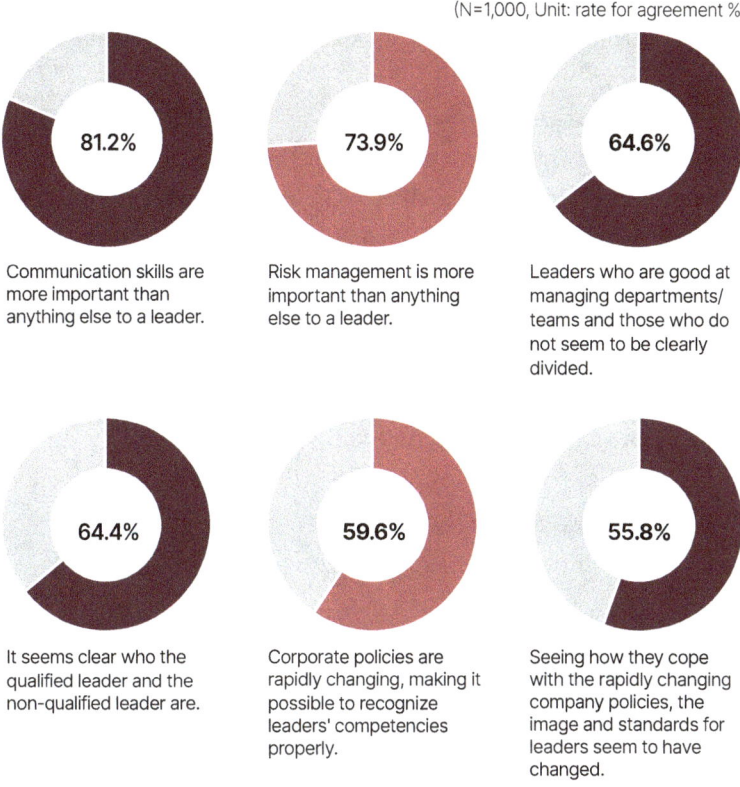

Source: Result of Embrain Research, perceptions of leaders inside the organization after changes in the working environment caused by COVID-19 (2020)

important, while 68.7% of the respondents said that the role of leaders will become more important in the post-COVID era. 81.2% of the respondents said, "I realized that communication is more important than anything else to leaders in the COVID era," and 73.9% agreed that risk management competency is essential. As a result, it was found that efficient communication in a non-face-to-face environment is the most crucial leadership competency; and the competency to effectively respond to a rapidly changing business environment is also emphasized as an essential leadership competency.

Along with the five competencies (digital communication, data management, data analytics, content production, and change management), leaders also need to be equipped with new virtual leadership competencies, such as digital communication (feedback, coaching), risk management, non-face-to-face performance management, and collaboration/problem-solving competencies in a non-face-to-to-face working environment.

Of course, these competencies were necessary for sales leaders even before COVID-19, but they could not be considered essential for all organizations. However, in the COVID era, sales leaders must develop and foster these competencies.

The competencies that sales leaders need during the COVID-19 era

1. **Digital communication (Feedback, coaching)**
   The competency to effectively communicate with organizational members to suit the non-face-to-face environment, and lead team meetings, offer feedback and coaching based on different situations in a non-face-to-face environment (including document-based communication)

2. **Risk management**
   The competency to predict, prepare for, and effectively respond to risks in advance in a rapidly changing business environment

3. **Non-face-to-face performance management**
   The competency to set strategic goals to fit the COVID era and operate and manage organizations (organizational resources) to maximize performance

4. **Collaboration/problem-solving in a non-face-to-face environment**
   The competency to resolve problems through collaboration within the department or with other departments in a non-face-to-face environment

In the New Normal era, sales coaching & non-face-to-face communication

For sales, external factors such as COVID-19 can be found anytime. Sales team leaders should make predictions in advance, and adapt quickly to changing situations to lead the department stably—instead of panicking over changes in the external environment. How should sales leaders coach their members? Let's look at it through a specific example.

CASE STORY 4
'The telecommuting issue' in the post-COVID era

Team leader H, of a vehicle parts manufacturing Company L, had an embarrassing experience with their client company during a meeting. Initially, it was a video meeting to explain the new product, and C was the assistant manager in charge of the businesses related to this client company. Due to a problem with C's laptop, team leader H had to try to explain the products directly. However, the product explanation session did not proceed as it should have, since the online meeting was conducted through a platform internally used in the client company instead of video conferencing tools everyone was familiar with. Fortunately, the client company had been doing business with Company L for a long time. Hence, H asked for their understanding and rescheduled the meeting. Still, H was worried about having shown inexperience in front of the client company and team members. In particular, H was more concerned with emphasizing the importance of getting used to video conferencing tools, and mastering the majority of tools commonly used in the market when giving feedback to the team members. Moreover, as the team has not been able to hold face-to-face meetings with all the members recently, the difficulty of adequately identifying issues and ineffective communication among team members has been a concern.

The following is a partial adaptation of the interview with C, a sales assistant manager of Company L, who telecommutes and works from home.

Writer How do you conduct your work these days?
Assistant Manager C The sales team is taking turns to work from home.
Writer Could you talk about the pros and cons of remote work?
Assistant Manager C The pros are that the commuting time has been reduced, and we can work in comfortable clothes. The downside is that we do not have access to some documents needed for our client meetings, due to security restrictions. And recently, online meetings have been increasing, but using various online conferencing tools is challenging. In some cases, customers

were more proficient in using the tools, making me nervous during the meeting; in other cases, I had to spend the whole meeting explaining how to use the tool to customers who didn't know how to use Zoom or Teams at all. Also, there were cases where the meeting didn't proceed smoothly, because something with the laptop went wrong during the session. I think it's vital to be able to respond fast to all kinds of different circumstances.

Writer This must be causing some inconvenience in the working process. Are there any other problems?

Assistant Manager C The problems I mentioned earlier are improving, as both our customers and we are getting used to the situation, but the most frustrating thing is that it is hard to communicate with the management.

Writer Why is that?

Assistant Manager C The management seems frustrated when they cannot directly see the salespeople. They told me to always turn on the company's instant messaging app when working from home. When the calls with customers run over, I receive calls and texts asking what I am doing at home, since the management saw my status changed to unavailable on the messaging app. And with remote work, before ending my job for the day, I have to write and submit what I did today on an hourly basis. But the problem is, there is not much to write about, even though I did work hard. That's why I'm forced to make up work. I often feel monitored and watched while working from home, and I think this is why many employees prefer to work in the office. In the past, we used to receive feedback while having meetings in person and having a drink, but in a non-face-to-face environment, the management and salespeople both find it hard to give and receive feedback directly.

Writer The management probably prefers face-to-face meetings… What else? Is there any other issue?

Assistant Manager C Another problem is that adapting appropriately to the changing environment is challenging. The company does not want the leaders just to manage and receive reports like before. The company desires experience-based leaders, to lead the team with horizontal leadership, but our team leader still tends to work vertically like before. Of course, the team leader has changed much compared to the past. Oh, and the team leader is not good at handling video conferencing tools or other IT packages, and only gives instructions to us to practice and master those tools. Hence, our trust in our leader starts to reduce. Regarding those technical problems, the team leader may not be as good as younger employees, but we look forward to the leader's efforts.

As more and more companies choose remote work, the salespeople's work satisfaction has decreased, as can be seen in the interview above. In addition, as customers are reluctant to be visited by salespeople, the value of salespeople's existence is being questioned as the number of sales legwork, which was previously a primary task for salespeople, naturally decreases. In the meantime, some team leaders are trying to control their salespeople. When salespeople lose autonomy, they tend to be trapped in a self-defensive state, instead of trying to find new sales approaches with a growth mindset. Hence, leaders' non-face-to-face communication competency can significantly influence their employees' motivation and commitment to work.

So, what do the sales leaders who manage these salespeople think? We try to understand their thoughts through an interview with Company L's sales team leader, H. The interview below is partially adapted for clarity.

Writer I heard that the company's salespeople are taking turns working from home due to COVID-19. What do you think about remote work?

Team Leader H It is understandable that there is no choice but to work from home due to COVID-19, but I think it's inevitable that it's less efficient than working from the office.

Writer: What makes it less efficient, specifically?

Team Leader H I'm having a hard time communicating with the employees. In the past, when we met and talked in person, I think the employees understood my intentions better. It was also easy for me to get a grasp of how well the employees understood what I said. But now that we're communicating online, miscommunications are inevitable. And honestly, it is hard to comprehend precisely what kind of work the employees are doing at home, which is frustrating.

Writer Then, how do you plan to resolve these problems?

Team Leader H To prevent employees from doing anything else but work at home, we require our employees to keep the company's instant messaging app on during working hours. The employees also need to submit their daily work log, to help accurately understand what kind of work they are doing. If possible, I have the employees write their work log hourly and submit it, but it's hard to assert the authenticity of the work log... I think this is why I consistently ask about their work during online team meetings or 1:1 meetings.

Both sales leaders and salespeople are under stress due to the recent increase in telecommuting and shrinking sales activities due to COVID-19. Therefore, it can be said that the competencies of sales leaders have become more critical; what attitude should leaders adopt to manage salespeople's performance while helping the department to keep innovating?

Sales Leader's Coaching: escape from experience-based habitual thinking

The following is an experiment conducted by a psychologist.

> A soldier and an old man were talking on the sidewalk, and a child ran to the soldier breathing hard, saying, "Your father and my father are fighting." The old man asked the soldier, "Do you know this child?" The soldier replied, "He's my son." Then, what is the relationship between the soldier and the two people who are now fighting?

The answer is as follows. The soldier is the child's mother, and the people in the fight are the father and grandfather on the mother's side of the child. Surprisingly, only two out of 100 people in this experiment answered correctly. If you have answered correctly, you are extraordinary and you made it to the 2%.

The psychologist who conducted the experiment, later visited a family and asked them the same question. Only a little kid was able to give the correct answer. Most adults got it wrong. The reason is that we are stuck in stereotypes based on our past experiences. This is called the 'phenomenon of experience-based habitual thinking.' Experience-based habitual thinking refers to a psychological tendency to react or respond habitually after a particular stimulus occurs. Only a few adults could correctly answer this question, because they were pretty sure that the soldier should be a man based on their experiences.[3]

We are much more caught up in our past experiences than we think. In addition, as you get older, people tend to rely more on past experiences. The same applies to the management and sales sectors. Leaders with a lot of successful experiences are more likely to show a tendency to find solutions from past experiences when they come across a problem, thinking, "Was there a similar problem in the past? How did I resolve it then?" Experiences are significant in sales. This is because past experiences incorporate methods such as how to lead a customer consultation, how to get a grasp of customers' needs, and how to dominate the psychological warfare at the negotiation table. The problem is that this empirical attitude leads to habitual thinking. Moreover, for an organization to survive in a changing era, the leaders' successful sales experiences should no longer be considered a pearl of wisdom. Instead, it is becoming more important to escape from the existing offline-based sales processes or methodology, pick up new sales approaches, and personalize these with your own experiences to create solutions in response to the post-COVID era. This is why we should not be obsessed only with past experiences and successes.

In a non-face-to-face era, competitors' sales departments are pursuing organizational innovation by considering ways to approach customers more effectively, while thinking from the customer's point of view by utilizing various non-face-to-face approaches. In this case, if leaders are obsessed with past experiences, and insist on conducting offline meetings with customers, the organization will fall behind in competition and be shunned by customers who crave change.

So, what should sales leaders do under the circumstances? Leaders should be the first to promote agility, aka the adaptability to stand at the center of change and lead it.

> We collated adaptability with agility based on the agile methodology, which means 'pursuing change in response to the market quickly.'

In addition, flexibility must also be utilized in order to deal with uncertainty. In the past, to succeed in sales, it was challenging to invest plenty of time in offline activities, to find customers and establish relationships. Now, it is crucial to quickly provide customized information to clients anytime, anywhere, and prepare for sales in online situations. In this case, the sales team's way of working should be closer to an agile approach with increased flexibility, instead of course development and operations. The critical points that sales departments operating in an agile environment should pursue are quick responses, hyper-personalization, and efficiency.

Organizations must evolve to survive in a constantly changing business environment, with the emergence of pandemics like COVID-19, and the sudden shift in how competitors operate. However, while most organizational members know the need for change, they believe that "people around me, or team members in other departments, will need to change, instead of me." In other words, as individuals, organizational members want to be excluded from the change. However, when the external environment changes as rapidly as it does now, discoveries and innovations should be sought instead of relying on the past. In other words, leaders should not try to contain change and do the same things that they have done well until now, but search for, and adapt to, what they should do. Thus, we came up with three questions that sales leaders should ask themselves. These questions will serve as a starting point for innovating the sales department, and an opportunity to help realize more efficient and effective sales.

> **The critical points that sales teams should pursue in the post-COVID era**
>
> **1. Quick Response**
> In a non-face-to-face online environment, customers approach with more options than in an offline environment. Hence, the sales team needs to respond faster.
>
> **2. Hyper-personalization**
> Salespeople should respond with services tailored to the customers' preferences. Customers should not be treated based on the same standard as in the past. Customers should be approached with the channel they prefer and the way they want.
>
> **3. Efficiency During**
> During non-face-to-face sales, efficient procedures are more likely to be achieved than in offline sales. You must shift offline activities online, test them out quickly, and adopt an approach that continuously increases efficiency.

Q1. Are our sales approaches appropriate for today's customers?

As times change, customers' lifestyles and work patterns change; our sales approach naturally changes accordingly. The changing pattern has gradually shifted from face-to-face to non-face-to-face communication, from documents to videos, and from PCs to mobile phones. However, due to COVID-19, the speed of change is progressing dramatically and rapidly. While our customers are also changing in response to the external environment, we will have to think about whether our sales approaches reflect the changes or not. To change our way of conducting sales, we will have to read the customer's lifestyle first. We should compare and check our sales approaches simultaneously with the customers' preferences, to see if we are asking for face-to-face meetings with customers who are working from home, printing and showing dozens of pages of proposals to customers who are more familiar with video-based information delivery, and whether the information we provide is legible on a mobile phone.

Now our customer diversity varies, including both customers who still pursue the previous sales approaches, and customers who seek the latest systems and communication methods in response to the new era. Salespeople should strive to meet these diverse customer needs when conducting sales activities. Sales leaders should not hesitate to thoroughly examine their customers, and introduce various sales methods tailored to customers' preferences. The focus here is that you must respond flexibly to the customer's situation. And the key is to practice a customer-centric sales approach.

Q2. Am I sensitive to change and ready to accept new things?
Earlier in this book, we talked about 'change blindness.' Indeed, you need to make sure you are sensitive to the changes around you. When you look at the sales leaders' awareness and sensitivity to change, most are aware of specific changes within their industries or personal interests; changes in other areas are often overlooked. For example, the marketing leader of the cell phone industry is well aware of information related to their work, such as Apple and Samsung's latest launch of phones and the latest trend for mobile phones, as well as information about personal hobbies, like the

trend for golf course green fee. On the other hand, this marketing leader may not be interested in the increase in non-face-to-face meetings due to COVID-19, the pros and cons of various tools utilized during online sessions, and the corresponding changes in global conference call equipment companies. But are the cell phone industry and online meeting industry irrelevant? You could have thought so in the past, but now many people have meetings on their tablets, smartphones, and laptops. Taking this into account, it is a necessary competency for sales/marketing leaders to test out various online meeting tools, and apply things that are relevant to the marketing of smartphones. Who knows? A few years later, cars might be sold in the same market as smartphones. At that time, a leader who prepares ahead of time, and proactively adapts to change, will be able to sell both smartphones and cars better than anyone else.

Q3. Am I constantly learning?

Change does not end with the recognition of change. To accept and adapt to changes, leaders need to learn constantly. Steve Jobs, who led Apple's innovation, said in an interview in 1984, "If I were an outstanding talent, would I want to work for somebody I can't learn anything from?" This is why Steve Jobs chose to train experts and promote them to the management, instead of directly hiring the management externally; therefore, to this day, Apple's leadership is still made up of people who can work in the field that they have expertise in, and cooperate with their colleagues during the decision-making process. Likewise, sales leaders will be qualified to lead only when they possess expertise in their field. In the past, people with outstanding performance, or extensive successful sales experiences, were evaluated as experts in sales, but now past wisdom no longer guarantees expertise. A desirable sales leader recognizes potential customers and changes in the market ahead of others, and proactively tests out and utilizes new technologies or approaches relevant to sales departments, to respond to and lead the change.

Non-face-to-face communication of sales leaders: communicate constantly with team members

Baek Jong-won, a franchise restaurant owner and culinary researcher, starred in a Korean TV show called Alley Restaurant. The program featured casts with various problems, ranging from a restaurant owner who was too unprepared for even essential dishes, to an owner who was extremely passionate about cooking but had no business sense. Most of them soon turned into great restaurants with the help of Baek Jong-won and the production team; some even grew bigger by maximizing the efficiency of their restaurant menus. However, when people visited those restaurants six months to a year later, they often saw that many had forgotten their promises to Baek Jong-won during the show, and had returned to their original operations.

Why did they still return to their original operations, even though Baek Jong-won has shown them all the tricks based on his accumulated experiences for operating successful restaurants, such as coaching them with business know-how and actively helping them develop recipes? Is it Baek's problem? I don't think that is necessarily the case. Even before Baek Jong-won's Alley Restaurant, there was a program called Solution! I See Money, which shared the experiences and know-how of popular restaurants with relatively more minor ones. And the same also happened to numerous restaurants in this program. After starring on the show, they shined for a while, but many fell back to their original modus operandi.

Why did this happen? We found the answer while offering consulting services to global pharmaceutical companies. While diagnosing the competencies of sales leaders at Company A, a Korean subsidiary of a global pharmaceutical company, investigated which competencies or actions of leaders had the most significant impact on the sales team's performance. Before conducting the survey, various competencies such as leaders' expertise, strategic planning, and communication were expected to affect the sales performance. Still, the team's performance did not go up just because the leader performed better in the scope of these competencies. According to the survey, two figures were proportional to the team's performance: sales leaders' number of coaching sessions (communication) and the achievement rate compared to the target customer visits.

Some sales leaders achieved their team's sales goals even if they communicated with less effective approaches, or lacked expertise and the competency to plan strategies. But without team leaders' coaching (communication), none of the teams could achieve their goals.

The same is true of the restaurants that starred in Baek Jong-won's Alley Restaurant mentioned above. If Baek Jong-won and his production team had constantly visited, inspected, and modified for improvement even after the TV show, those restaurants would not have returned to their previous operations. They would have continued providing quality food and services. Earlier, based on Embrain's survey results, we confirmed that a communication competency is essential for leaders in the COVID era. Leaders now need to conduct coaching, that is, periodically discuss problems with corresponding solutions, and actively explore improvement plans when issues arise.

Then, how should sales leaders communicate with their members during the COVID era?

The correlation between the visit achievement rate and the performance achievement rate compared to the goal	Correlation between coaching scores (coaching frequency + amount) and performance achievement rate

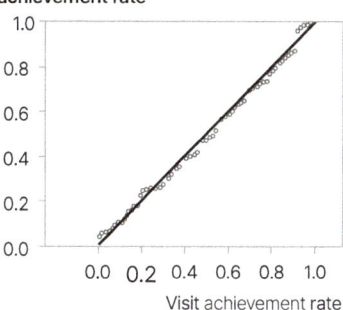

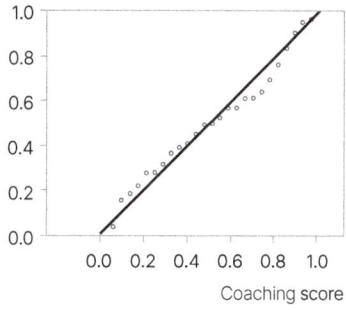

- As a result of analyzing the correlation of performance achievement, there was a significant correlation between the visit achievement rate and the performance achievement rate compared to the goal.

- Comparing the performance achievement rates of the top 20% and bottom 20% over the past three years, the top 20% (105%) was found to have a performance achievement rate of about 10% higher than the bottom 20% (102%).

- There is a significant correlation between the monthly salespeople coaching score (coaching frequency + amount) and the performance achievement rate. In other words, while coaching members, performance-related results tend to increase generally.

Source: Results of the correlation analysis between the global pharmaceutical company A's leader competencies and performance

Most employees routinely exchanged daily conversations in the office in the morning, and as an extension of these conversations, sales leaders' coaching and feedback-giving were naturally conducted. However, after COVID-19, even daily conversations became something sales leaders had to make time to do consciously. In other words, it is necessary to intentionally invest time in communicating with team members, and starting a personal conversation with each employee. In particular, the importance of such communication skills is expected to remain unchanged even after COVID ends.

According to a study conducted by the Boston Consulting Group and KRC Research, commissioned by Microsoft in 15 countries across Europe, the introduction of a flexible working system, which was only at 15% before COVID-19, has expanded to 76% of companies after COVID-19. 88% of the respondents predicted that a hybrid work model would continue to be applied, even after the COVID-19 pandemic.[4] In other words, communication will remain the most critical competency for leaders, because the future work model will not be much different from now.

So what should be done to solve communication problems, which are the biggest problem of remote work, and improve coaching competency?

First, leaders should stop giving instructions and providing solutions based on their limited experiences, and start to coach in terms of facilitating. As mentioned, unlike in the past, coaching based on open learning encourages individual team members to coach in the area where they possess the most expertise and experience, in contrast to one-sided coaching delivered by team leaders. The best coaching in a non-face-to-face environment is leading team members to find the most suitable approach in various situations, that is, a facilitating type of coaching. This means that the

Communication approaches for coaching in a non-face-to-face environment[5]

1. Sales leaders conduct conference calls two to three times a week when necessary. When running a video conference, instead of giving notice of the scheduled time, proceed at the time when all participants are available, considering the schedule of the team members.

2. Unlike offline meetings, it is difficult for multiple people to talk simultaneously during video conferences. This is because messages may not be clearly delivered if the voice is received simultaneously. Therefore, sales leaders must pre-set the topics and corresponding orders and share them accordingly.

    * When conducting a video conference, it is beneficial to remember the following 3Ps. Purpose (of video conferencing(the purpose of communication)), Process (the order of proceeding the meeting (the proper order to speak)), and Payoff (the result of the meeting, the expected results, the establishment of a to-do list)

3. Unlike offline, reading one's facial expressions or intentions may be challenging. Therefore, leaders should actively utilize functions such as chatting or anonymous voting. Particularly in Korea, everyone tends to be quiet when asked to give opinions. Thus, the leader must actively draw the team members out if necessary. As an additional procedure, leaders should consider conducting 1:1 meetings with introverted employees.

4. Written communication should also be actively utilized. When conducting video conferences, things may get missed. It is time to actively coach and deliver feedback that has

not yet been communicated via e-mail or other messengers. Also, leaders should consider the preferences of employees that some employees favor written communication over phone calls. In particular, if work needs improvement, it is necessary to accurately deliver the message more carefully instead of using an offline approach. In this case, written communication can be utilized. Instead of criticizing adversely, leaders should lead the conversation, find solutions with their team members, and proactively communicate and provide hints.

5. If there is anything to celebrate or praise, it is recommended to actively utilize gifting apps like gifticon and coupons to express wishes and appreciation. Leaders should remember that to intrinsically motivate their employees in a non-face-to-face environment, it is necessary to make them feel capable of the job and belongingness.

6. Immediate responses should not be expected. Sometimes, leaders may have to talk alone for more than 10 or 20 minutes during a meeting. Therefore, questions should be asked here and there to test out team members' reactions.

7. Finally, it is necessary to ask the team members if they need help, cooperation, and coordination during sales or work. Something that can be easily overlooked is that in a non-face-to-face environment, leaders should make more efforts to coordinate with other departments. A leader's competency to collaborate and resolve problems can be directly related to the performance of their team members.

approach and solution should also vary depending on the person who receives the coaching.

Second, it is necessary to support team members to become familiar with various tools for collaborative work in a non-face-to-face environment. Sales leaders should proactively manage relationships with their members and help them to find the most comfortable way to communicate with each other, in addition to simply sending emails or having video meetings through Zoom. And team members can choose tools and communication styles that suit them better, when offered diversified options and flexibility. Moreover, salespeople should know how to use and freely switch among multiple tools, because they must adapt to various means depending on their customers' preferences.

Third, educating team members on how to communicate remotely is necessary. Team leaders should notice that their team members may not be familiar with the diverse online communication methods that other departments or employees are trying to test. Therefore, educating and supporting the team members to have the competency of producing and utilizing content in a non-face-to-face environment is essential.

The following figure is part of K Pharmaceutical Company's non-face-to-face sales competency enhancement program. K Pharmaceutical Company has strengthened salespeople's competencies through various training, so that salespeople can conduct remote communication with customers more professionally. In particular, this program has been organized to enable the salespeople to have critical efficient sales competencies, which are needed in a non-face-to-face environment within a short period, including appearance management and attitude, verbal communication and speech skills, and IT expertise.

Lastly, leaders should establish a communication method and consistently continue their daily communication with team members. Organizations with regular routines such as team meetings, town hall meetings, 1:1 reviews, and brainstorming sessions were more effective in remote work than those that were not. To continue this, leaders must consider the employees' preferred communication methods instead of planning the meeting and forcing participation. It will be an opportunity to check each organizational member's current level of knowledge and which communication method is more effective.

The example of K Pharmaceutical Company's non-face-to-face sales competency enhancement program

Professional Visual	Professional Attitude	Professional Communication	Professional IT Expertise
The visual factor that determines the first impression of a professional	A professional attitude that focuses on customers	Key actions that convey expertise through interaction	IT competencies that lead the changing work environment
Smart Image Making Professional image-making for an image-driven era		**Professional Virtual Call I: Non-face-to-face consulting competency** Optimized environmental settings for Virtual Calls and methods for successful consulting	
		Professional Virtual Call II: Ways to approach customers by customer types Increase Virtual Call success rate based on customer interest and skill proficiency	
		Engaging Speech Speak decently and with speech skills suitable in a digital environment	
		Presentation Skill-up Individual virtual PPT skills that increase the presentation success rate	
		Smart Text Communication More important written communication skills in a non-face-to-face environment	

'Fostering/coaching' points that sales leaders should think of in the New Normal era

Earlier, we looked at the role and competencies of sales leaders in the post-COVID era, and how they can better communicate and coach their team members. Now, we will discuss leadership-related points that leaders should consider in the post-COVID age.

Open learning vs. Enclosed learning

A professor showed his students a list of cards with the numbers 2, 4, and 6 appearing in order. Then, the students were asked to guess what the rules were for the numbers that would appear next. Students who participated in the experiment had to answer only by presenting the following numbers that would fit these rules. And although they could mention as many numbers as they wanted, the rules had to be presumed correctly. The majority of students said the number 8, and the professor hinted, "Don't keep your eye on the rules." The students then gave numbers 10, 12, and 14, but each time the professor answered, "Don't keep your eye on the rules." Then, a student spoke out on behalf of the class, "Professor, the rule is to add 2 to the last number." But the professor said the correct answer was not the rule. The students were quick to jump to conclusions.

But one student took a completely different approach. The student first called the number 4 and looked at the professor's reaction. The professor said, "Be aware of the rules." The student asked, "If so, is it 7?" The professor again said, "Don't keep your eye on the rules." The student called several different numbers, deliberately attempting to reach the wrong answer. 24, 9, 43. The student then answered, after sufficient testing, "Professor, the rule is that the next number must be greater than the previous number."

That was the correct answer. Many students answered incorrectly, but how did this student get the right solution? There was only one difference. Other students tried to get the correct answer according to the theory or experience in their heads, but this student deliberately took the wrong approach, conducted various tests, and tried something new.[6]

This test was an experiment on the confirmation bias commonly held by people. Confirmation bias means not accepting new information because we think our existing theories, worldviews, experiences, and knowledge are correct. In the post-COVID era, everything is bound to be unique. Suppose sales leaders prioritize an enclosed learning approach based only on past experiences, and disregard new tools or methodologies. In that case, they will fail to lead their sales teams in a new environment. What sales leaders need in the post-COVID era is an open learning attitude to accept new things actively, and to learn and share those things if team members show excellent competencies (better than their leaders).

Approaches to maximize Productivity vs. Creativity

Israeli psychologist Michael Bar-Eli and his colleagues conducted an interesting experiment on elite football players. It was an experiment on which direction the goalkeepers move when blocking the penalty kick. During a penalty kick, the goalkeeper analyzes the usually preferred movement for each kicker, or as soon as the kicker kicks the ball, the goalkeeper predicts the direction of the kick by looking at the stepping foot. This is because the ball cannot be blocked if the goalkeeper moves after seeing which direction the kicker kicks. However, interesting results came out when we analyzed 286 penalty kicks in the world's best leagues and championships. In terms of probability, the optimal strategy for the goalkeeper was to stay in the center of the goal, but in reality, the goalkeeper often jumped to the right or left. In the following table, the kicker chose the left, center, and right almost evenly, but it can be seen that the goalkeeper's jump direction is mainly to the left or right.

The kick direction and the goalkeeper's jump direction

		Goalkeeper's jump direction			
		Left	Center	Right	Total
Kick direction	Left	18.9%	0.3%	12.9%	32.2%
	Center	14.3%	3.5%	10.8%	28.7%
	Right	16.1%	2.4%	20.6%	39.2%
	Total	49.3%	6.3%	44.4%	100.0%

According to the classical assumptions of economics, when facing decision-making problems with uncertainties, people have to choose what to do by considering the probability distribution of the expected outcome. Therefore, in some cases, it may be a better decision to take no action. However, the problem is that everyday decision-making is not realized based on this logic. The issue of action bias arises: taking action, even if it is of no use.[7]

Sales leaders in the post-COVID era will also likely succumb to action bias. Leaders should focus on solving problems by delegating work to team members in a non-face-to-face environment, and resolving issues when they arise. However, unnecessary video conferencing or reporting is carried out, under the pressure of at least having to do something during telecommuting situations. They want to find some comfort by working a tight schedule, and thinking they are increasing their working productivity.

When conducting human resources consulting to calculate the appropriate staffing to increase organizational productivity, people often make the same mistake. A generic method of calculating the right workforce is to analyze each individual's job and working hours, and measure how productive work is performed based on a 100% scale. Principally, this approach may be efficient for routine tasks or pre-organized tasks. However, sales activities involve customer meetings and consultation with uncertainties; a more creative approach is required. In this case, it is not easy to measure productivity using the same markers. The point that leaders need to think about is the perception of productivity.

The following puzzle shows that the perception of productivity is not always correct. The goal of this game is to move the number blocks by utilizing the empty block to match them in order. But what if we remove the empty block from this puzzle? Since the empty space disappears, space utilization is maximized.

Tom DeMarco's Puzzle Metaphor8

7	1	6
4	8	3
2	5	

▶

7	1	6
4	8	3
2	5	9

But what if we fill up our work schedule like this? Productivity will be at 100%, but flexibility will decrease, as space cannot be utilized differently. And the organizational tension and stress will also increase. Suppose organizational leaders try to check their members' every move in a non-face-to-face environment, and increase productivity by 100%. In that case, the side effects of increasing organizational tension may also come along. On the contrary, leadership suitable for the current era encourages brand new sales activities, while allowing members to think outside the box and engage in creative activities instead of improving productivity by controlling them. The flexibility and agility of the sales department can also be increased when leaders break away from the obsession of "Let's at least do something!" and "Let's try it first and see!"

Control the information vs. Share the information

"Non-face-to-face" and "remote work" are keywords that have become the hottest topic in the workplace after COVID-19. As this non-face-to-face and remote work become a daily occurrence, one of the most significant changes is the flow of information. In the past, it was common for teams to spread necessary information through leaders. Since only a specific number of people attended offline meetings, important information was generally provided to leaders first, and then shared with team members. As a result, information asymmetry naturally arose. In economics, information asymmetry refers to a structural information imbalance, in which each entity in the market differs in the amount of information held. Due to this information imbalance, those with more information possess power and advantages. The most representative case is the used car market. Used car dealers have more information on vehicles than consumers, so based on that information, they can sell and benefit from selling cars in conditions that are more favorable to them.

In the past, for leaders, such information asymmetry served to occupy the market power and advantageous market positions. This is because having more information leads to using it to benefit one's work. However, there is a high risk that information will flow negatively in a non-face-to-face environment. For example, if leaders do not share information with team members, and keep it only to themselves, the members will not be able to know this information. And they will not be able to proceed with their work correctly, which will inevitably slow the progress. The slower the sharing of information, the higher the likelihood of errors during organizational decision-making, or business processing.

General Stanley A. McChrystal, former commander of the JSOC[Joint Special Operations Command] in Iraq, says in his book Team of

Teams that in the military, where information security is as vital as life, he instead felt the importance of information sharing. As everyone knows, information is of crucial importance in the military. In particular, confidentiality and security within special forces that conduct special operations using unconventional techniques are more critical. However, ironically, the Special Operations Command leader emphasizes the importance of information sharing. In the past, information was something that had to be highly protected, and only shared with specific people as needed. However, with the arrival of the information explosion era, various systems are becoming more complex, so it has become difficult to determine who needs what information. In addition, complaints arose among special troops working in the field that information was not properly shared. He talked about the need for change as follows: "We have to change the culture related to information. We have to break down the wall and share it. We have to focus on 'Who doesn't know?' instead of 'Who should know.' And we have to tell everyone, as soon as possible. This will be an essential cultural change for organizations with many secrets."

No place controls information and pursues efficiency more than the military. However, McChrystal says that communication and information sharing are even more critical, since you cannot be sure about everything that happens in a complex and chaotic environment. He also explains why more communication and information sharing are essential through the concept of the "wavelength" of tasks. And as shown in the figure below, the commander, equivalent to a company's executives responsible for strategic decisions, has a longer wavelength. Because they see the big picture, and think deeper at a slower pace. However, the closer you get to the practitioner in the field, the shorter the wavelength of your work.

Comparing the wavelength of tasks to the military, the established strategy is sequentially spread to intermediate military organizations (battalion, squadron) and small military units in combat orders. Companies establish mid- to long-term strategies, and spread them from the group up to each individual. However, McChrystal says that more frequent information sharing and subsequent delegation of authority are important, because things can change over time. The point he wants to emphasize here is not a top-down approach of checking and commanding as in the past, but conversations. In addition, all members must perform tasks functionally and proactively. Ultimately, the open environment and democratization of information he emphasizes are the primary keys to making everything work in an uncertain environment.

| The "Wavelength" of Tasks

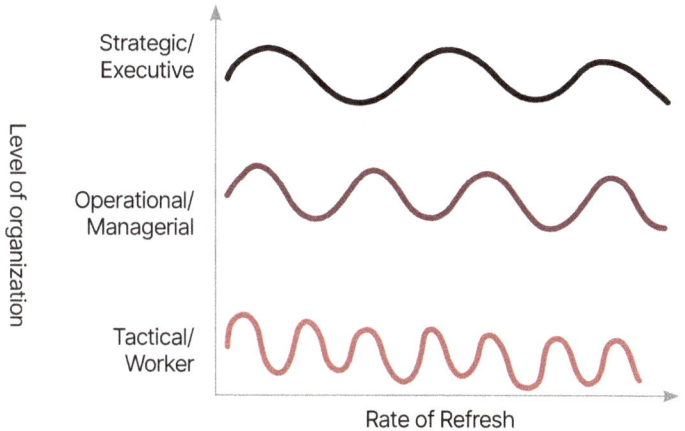

Source: Deloitte University Press|DUPress.com

The fact that sales leaders should not control and monopolize information as in the past in a non-face-to-face environment is similar to what General McChrystal says about the military. If work is done remotely, and the leader cannot directly witness the working process, information sharing within the team must be smooth enough to enable faster and proper decision-making. Sometimes, the leader may delegate members' authority to make decisions and then report to the leader.

So, how should leaders share information in a non-face-to-face environment? You can get a hint from General McChrystal's "O&I: Operations and Intelligence Meeting," held in Iraq. He held meetings with 2,000 troops, 6 days a week and 2 hours a day, to share information. At 9 a.m. in Washington, U.S., and 4 p.m. in Iraq, the entire headquarters participated in two hours of information sharing through video, anywhere in the world. O&I was open to everyone who wanted to get or share information. It was a democratic information-sharing meeting where anyone, from generals to soldiers, could offer updates and ask questions. Of course, 2 hours was relatively long, but anyone could freely participate. These two hours were critical due to the nature of the military, since they must master the battlefield environment information. (Since military operations are carried out 24 hours a day, it should be understood that their 2 hours are significantly different than that of a company.)

The characteristics of the O&I meeting are as follows:

1. Information can easily become outdated, so it should be shared quickly.
2. The person who best judges which information is valuable is the end user of the information.

3. The person who best understands the information is the user of that information.
4. The best way to understand information is to share and analyze information together.

Thanks to this information-sharing system introduced by McChrystal, the number of JSOC enemy raids increased from 10 per month to 300 per month. This was because it was easy to quickly make decisions, and grasp information about enemies, through information sharing.[8]

The key to information sharing is to communicate more often.

As we have seen earlier, both in Baek Jong-won's and the global pharmaceutical company's coaching case, leaders should communicate more and share information in a non-face-to-face environment. Leaders should not hold back information. While sharing information, there are two questions leaders should ask their team members.

1. What is your priority for this week?
2. How can I help?

It is essential to focus on employees' difficulties in the ongoing work, and on how the leaders should help resolve the problems instead of only checking their work. And the only thing leaders have to do is to acknowledge and understand team members' work priorities.[9]

Growth mindset vs. Fixed mindset

Not long ago, I watched a Korean entertainment program called Let's Play Basketball. The program was a sequel to We Kick Together, in which sports players from various national teams made fun episodes while playing soccer instead of their specialty sport. During the program, Huh Jae, who played for the soccer team of the previous program, became a coach, and Ahn Jung-hwan, who used to be a coach, appeared as a player. I want to introduce a scene that caught my eyes. In that scene, coach Huh Jae, who had struggled to play as a player, was coaching and guiding.

Coach Huh Jae emphasized defense by pointing out the poor players. That's where the problem appeared. Coach Huh Jae emphasized the 'Get Two' defense, but the players did not understand it because it was a basketball term they had never heard of. Kim Byung-hyun, a former baseball player, interpreted 'Get Two' as a 'Relay' (similar pronunciation in Korean) in baseball, and all the other players seemed puzzled because they didn't understand what Huh Jae said. In basketball, 'Get Two' defense is a fundamental term for one person to defend two players, but it was a very unfamiliar term for players from other sports. Here, we can identify two issues that often arise in the workplace. The first is 'recognition of change.' Head coach Huh Jae tried to lead the Let's Play Basketball team based on his previous experiences as a basketball coach, which was a mistake, since the environment, people, and players' competencies were different. Instead, what he needed to do was to quickly identify the changing environment, and establish strategies that fit this situation. The second is the 'importance of communication that fits the other party involved in the communication process.' Coach Huh Jae communicated based on his stance and perspectives, without considering other team members—and failed to put himself in other members' shoes. Of course, these were expressed in a more pronounced way because it was an entertainment show, but we could say it's similar to the COVID-19 situation.

During the COVID period, leaders must communicate more carefully than before, taking their team member's perspectives more into account. In particular, leaders should be able to grasp and understand what kind of non-face-to-face environments the team members are in, since their working environments can be very different from one another. Sometimes, video meetings are tricky because some employees are with their children, and others may find it challenging to work, since they have to be in the same space with their families. In addition, sales activities may be required to be conducted in a completely different environment, depending on the region or product line the salespeople are in charge of. There are more things that leaders should consider and ruminate over.

At this time, what is needed is a growth mindset. The theory of mindset is proposed by Carol S. Dweck, professor of psychology at Stanford University. The growth mindset believes that one's talents and abilities can be developed. and that anyone can grow their current ability through constant efforts, excellent strategies, and support and help from others. In other words, the growth mindset is to accept new things, with the idea that you can grow as much as you want even if the situation changes, and the status can change at any time. Both leaders and team members should recognize the changing environment, and utilize the mindset to grow through new learning. Leaders should also lead the change, with the belief and attitude that the team members can grow from the other person's point of view. On the contrary, a fixed mindset refers to believing that one's talents and abilities are immutable and fixed. No matter how hard someone tries, those factors cannot be changed.

For example, let's say that you've received an arduous project task. People with a fixed mindset quickly become frustrated and blame themselves for their lack of competencies, thinking that results cannot be produced even if they try. In the end, they think, "Well, that's just typical of me..." and give up. In contrast, even if people with a growth mindset fail, they try to overcome their weaknesses by thinking, "I can try again" or "I should try harder."

The field that has changed the most since the outbreak of COVID-19 may be the education sector. Of course, there have been many changes in other industries, but few have changed their way of working as much as education. Existing offline collective education has shifted to learning via non-face-to-face live classes or platforms, and students have lectures through Zoom instead of going to school. Therefore, those who gave lectures as their primary job had to undergo many changes. While there are instructors who naturally seek to change and develop themselves anew, there are instructors who naturally fall behind by sticking to the existing teaching methods. In particular, in the corporate education industry, quite a few instructors were looking for other jobs, saying they "could not handle new tools" such as Zoom or Teams. Because they have a fixed mindset, instead of a growth mindset, they could not make a guess or estimate the growth potential of the changing environment.

In contrast to younger employees, sales leaders are those who directly feel the hardness and trickiness experienced by the sales departments in the changing environment during COVID. Not long ago, I heard an interesting story at a meeting with the head of a group's education team. Since last year, live training has been conducted via Zoom instead of the existing collective education for executives and employees. And the response is unexpectedly positive, saying that non-face-to-face education will continue to be used even after COVID-19. According to a post-training survey, 80% of entry-level employees and assistant managers prefer non-face-to-face education via Zoom or other platforms, even when COVID-19 is over. However, managerial-level leaders had different opinions; only 45% said they liked non-face-to-face training. Leaders who have worked for more than 10 to 15 years may feel unfamiliar with the new communication approaches. This situation will not be different in sales. As we have seen earlier, the competencies required for sales departments in the COVID-19 era are entirely different, such as digital and content production competencies. Now, you will be able to achieve the same results as before COVID only when you shift to a growth mindset, and get used to new things while accepting changes.

CHECKLIST

Post-COVID era, sales leader's leadership/coaching and communication diagnosis table

Category	Checklist
The role and leadership of a sales leader	☐ Are you aiming for a coaching type of leadership based on a horizontal organizational culture?
	☐ Are you pursuing an agile organization and operations?
	☐ Do you consider the situation of each member according to the hyper-personalization issue?
The competencies of a sales leader during the COVID-19 era	☐ Do you possess the competency of effectively communicating with members in a non-face-to-face environment and leading the team meetings, giving feedback, and coaching in response to the current situation?
	☐ Can you predict, prepare, and effectively respond to risks ahead of time in a rapidly changing business environment?
	☐ Do you set strategic goals in response to the COVID-19 situation and operate and manage organizations (organizational resources) to maximize performance?
	☐ Do you possess the competency to resolve problems through cooperation and collaboration with your team members or other departments in a non-face-to-face environment?
Coaching, communication, and leader's mindset	☐ Are communication methods and tools suitable for a non-face-to-face environment introduced and applied?
	☐ Aren't you trapped in the past based on your experiences?
	☐ Does our sales department seek quick response_just in time, hyper-personalization_just for me, and efficiency_just enough?
	☐ Are you sensitive to change, and do you have a mind to learn constantly?
	☐ Do you give your members appropriate feedback and coaching in a non-face-to-face environment?
	☐ Are you actively sharing information instead of keeping it to yourself?
	☐ Are you continuing your efforts to maximize members' creativity and introduce new methodologies in the COVID-19 era?

Chapter 5

Sales New Normal #5
The operation of a sales department

In the New Normal era, what is the ideal way to operate a sales department?

🚩 Previously, we looked at various changes in how sales departments work, leadership, and organizational culture. However, it is necessary to consider not only how these sales departments work, soft skills, and leadership, but also the operations of sales departments. It may be beyond the scope of authority of sales leaders. Therefore, in this chapter, we would like to provide something to think about to sales leaders, management, and leadership in charge of the entire business unit. Of course, we will also discuss the challenges that sales leaders and members need to resolve. Let's think about what sales leaders should do, and how organizations should operate to enhance the performance of their sales department in the post-COVID era.

CASE STORY 5

A sales department's operations and transition of roles

* The story is based on an actual case, and some details/information have been changed.

Company A was a hidden champion who has built up solid technology in the healthcare industry for over 20 years. While continuing to accelerate growth, the company experienced unprecedented reverse growth due to COVID-19 in 2020, and is currently busy finding out solutions. As the situation worsens, there are conflicts within the organization between the strategy team in charge of the organizational strategy and the R&D department in charge of product planning, and the business division in charge of sales; that is, the conflict between the strategy and operation/implementation departments. Departments in charge of strategy and planning have previously complained that "The sales department has a lot of product-related requirements, only puts the blame on products, and fails to produce the results which should be delivered," and this kind of complaint has worsened due to COVID-19. On the contrary, the sales department is turning its back on the sluggish sales, saying, "In terms of the things that the sales department required and the changing market due to COVID-19, strategy and planning departments are not quickly giving relevant responses."

In particular, due to COVID-19, the sales department has been facing more and more challenges internally. Sales activities have not been actively carried out, compared to before COVID-19. Still, sales have not been decreasing significantly, so the challenges related to the roles of the sales department and the management have been strengthened.

Accordingly, the management formed an innovative TF team to

improve the working methods and business competencies, ensuring they're suitable for the COVID era. The head of the innovative TF team is the marketing team leader, who recently joined the company with a fresh perspective. Still, the members are composed of employees who have previously worked in each department, so that they can consider the interests of different departments when working.

Innovative TF team leader K started with the diagnosis of the existing organization. Understanding the current organization's way of working must come first to set up and promote new projects. As explained earlier, Company A is an equipment manufacturer with the world's No.1 technology. Since it was a global exporting company, the sales department was composed mainly of overseas sales teams, and the domestic market served as the test bed to firstly test out products manufactured by R&D.

Sales were mainly conducted through offline exhibitions, and the sales team focused on securing and managing dealers by participating in exhibitions more than ten times a year. However, since the region was divided and managed by the sales representatives, only the person in charge knew the issue or history of the corresponding area well. In addition, since sales tend to be actively conducted offline, online marketing, advertising, and PR activities were relatively not organically managed.

In the R&D department, developers were exclusively developing a single product, and as the company's operation was centered around R&D, a conflict arose between the R&D and sales departments. In addition, as developers' remuneration has improved in recent years, and the company even took special procedures in managing them, there has been a growing victim mentality that the sales department has been relatively alienated from the organization. Product development was carried out by applying ideas to the product, considering the needs of the market and dealers delivered by the sales, strategy, and marketing teams back to the R&D department. The problem was that, as the product was developed by reflecting the ideas of one or two planners, there were cases where the market needs were not adequately reflected, or the marketability was not analyzed.

Innovative TF team leader K also conducted interviews with members of each team. As a result, the biggest problem was the deepening conflict between the sales and planning departments.

Q. What improvements should the organization make in order to achieve results?

Sales Team Leader The problem is the strategy and R&D departments. Think about it. For equipment manufacturers like us, is there any other way more effective than going out and conducting sales activities? We actively go out to exhibitions and look for dealers. But does it make sense to say that we can't show the product at the exhibition immediately, just because of a schedule conflict with the developer, even though the customer badly wants to test it out? But it's frustrating that the company centers around the planning departments. Even though the sales department makes all the money. Last year was challenging because of COVID-19, but all companies were in similar situations. Customers were hesitant to place an order, so sales could not be generated. So, please consider and report the problems of the R&D department. If you look deeper, you will understand what I mean.

R&D Team Leader What did the sales team say? As you know, the organization's key is in development, strategy, and marketing. That's what the management and leadership say. Planning is done in the development and strategy departments, and operations and implementations are done in the sales department. The biggest problem is that the market response is not being delivered correctly to our department. The sales department only fragmentally provides and communicates the customers' inconveniences. But from the developing and improving products point of view, we can't immediately apply the inconvenience points that dealers discussed. Of course, I understand the sales department's perspectives, but let's consider the importance of our work. Honestly, salespeople should go out to conduct sales activities instead of just blaming the products. In addition, I try not to mention it, but these days, sales have not been adequately performing due to COVID-19. Even so, the sales department still has some sort of profit, so how should we interpret this?

Strategy Team Leader We have to coordinate the tasks of the entire company, and let the work proceed. Still, I think conflicts occur because each team has different interests, and a victim mentality is in action. Since the management emphasized strategy and development more, and told us that the sales team should only focus on simple implementation, the sales team tends to be alienated during the process. However, even if the management made such a decision, it was disappointing that the information was not organically shared within the organization. The strategy team may also be responsible for parts of it. Another problem is that it's hard to check each country's situation and customer responses, due to COVID-19.

Q. How are the sales achieved? How is the information being shared? And what efforts are made to obtain information?

Manager A of the Sales Team Sales is mainly done through dealers. We usually display products at large exhibitions, secure new dealers, or inform end product users in each region. When a customer inquiry comes from the website, a local representative will deliver it to the dealer. Then the dealer takes care of it. As for efforts made to get information, before going out to exhibitions, we usually put up a website banner through the agency in charge of the exhibitions. Data can be obtained through dealers or business trips, and sometimes through the customers we meet at exhibitions. Now, when it comes to information tracking, I am not very sure. As you know from the meetings you have experienced, even if we try to deliver the information we got, it feels that the information is not always adequately conveyed. So I don't think the data is being shared. Our team has an employee in charge of information sharing and exhibition reports, but I'm busy even managing dealers.

Q. How are you managing the exhibition information and dealers?

Manager B of the Sales Team Dealers regularly have meetings and conference calls on business trips abroad, or during exhibitions. They are systematically managed by region. If I have to pinpoint a problem, we usually share the reports after visiting the exhibition. But if the regional manager in charge is replaced, we have to check all the reports to know the history of each dealer. Indeed, information is not smoothly shared, because only regional managers continuously track and manage.

If you were K, how would you solve this problem?

Solution #1: Sales department, be an insider

Although the situation is different for each organization, the sales team in many companies has focused only on selling, as in the case of Company A above. Moreover, suppose you divide the strategy/planning and operation/implementation departments, like Company A does, and conduct business based on processes. In that case, you have no choice but to only perform your limited duties, depending on your role and responsibility. In the past, manufacturing-based and seller-oriented companies efficiently created and sold products based on processes. The producer focused only on making, and the seller focused only on selling. However, as we have seen earlier, this manufacturer-centered approach is no longer thriving in the COVID and VUCA era. Traditional processes do not work when customer needs and markets are diversified.

To solve the problem, the sales department should not stop at simply meeting customers outside and selling products. They should be an insider instead of an outsider within the organization. Here, insider means that they should spread information, and act as an information producer and disseminator that serves as the center of connection for each department.

The flow of information in the sales process is generally shown in the figure on the next page. For Company A's sales department to play a proper role, information secured at each sales stage must be well communicated to other departments, and thus be able to respond effectively to the market. And during the process, the sales department must play the role of the information center. When conducting organizational consulting of L, a leading manufacturing company in Korea, we investigated which department it was necessary to collaborate with, in order to improve the work performance of each department. According to the results, many departments in the company recognized the need for collaboration with the sales

The flow of information in the sales process

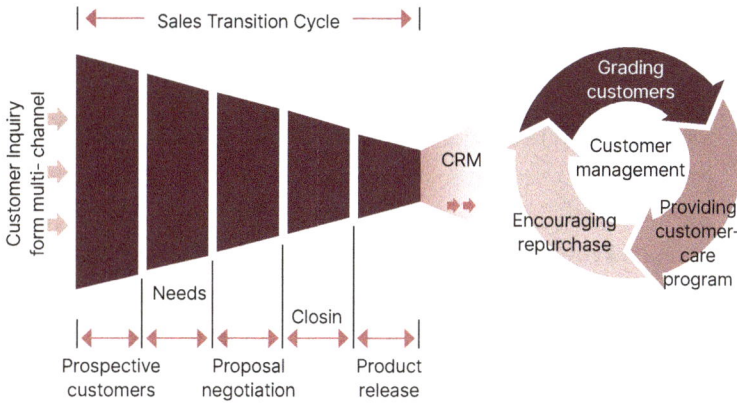

The map for Company L's needs for collaboration and diagnosis

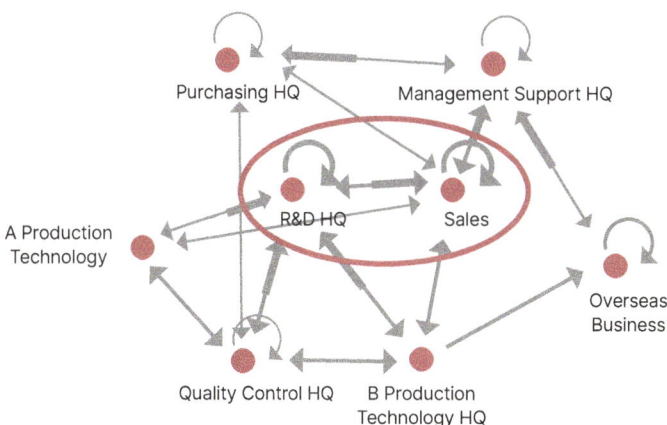

- The shape of a circle stands for each headquarter.
- Arrows indicate the relationship and direction of the needed collaboration
- The thickness of the arrow means the required amount of need.
- It is marked only when there are more than eight collaboration relationships among headquarters.

and R&D headquarters. In other words, for each organizational department to achieve better results while carrying out daily tasks or projects, it is essential to accurately identify and grasp the sales information, through actively communicating with the sales department and releasing and disseminating the product to the market based on their execution power.

Reason #1 why sales departments should become insiders and information disseminators: The visualization of information

Suppose a sales department like Company A is not at the center of communication. In that case, the information distribution among related departments in the company will be limited, and not smooth, even if consumer requirements $^{Voice\ of\ the\ Customer}$ or product issues arise. As a result, the same mistake will occur repeatedly, and

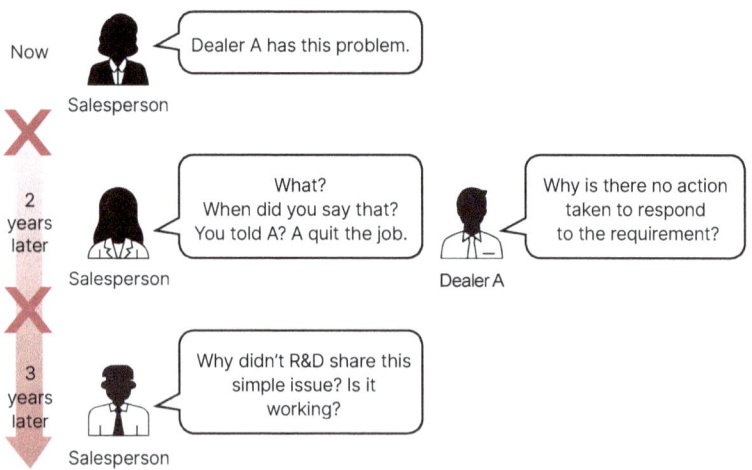

Problems that may arise in the absence of information visualization and feedback

the understanding of customers will keep reducing.

In addition, communication between the sales team and the support and production department is insufficient, and the prediction accuracy of the provided information is poor, which will lead to a failure to respond to the market demand appropriately, and the efficient operation of the workforce will be limited.

However, if the sales department becomes an insider, sales and marketing data can be collected and analyzed throughout the customers' pre-purchase phase, which is closely linked to development. In addition, the flow of information becomes smooth, so that the data can be used more visually. Eventually, all customer-related information is shared and analyzed, so it is possible to improve and develop products by utilizing the information as feedback.

As discussed earlier, Company A did not have a system to organize information into data and continuously share it. In addition, even if the information was obtained from exhibitions or specific dealers, no system allowed them to give feedback and share it. This can cause issues, as shown in the figure.

To solve such problems, it is necessary to share the information from various channels—such as exhibitions, dealers, and homepages—with the entire organization, and establish a system that enables the departments that are responsible for problem-solving, such as R&D and production departments, to deal with issues received from customers and share the results. In addition, data obtained from exhibitions and various marketing channels should be shared weekly or monthly through review meetings, to share the strengths and mistakes made, and resolve problems, improve, and develop. It is also vital to introduce a process for continuous learning, improving, and developing the organization, by regularly conducting review meetings—similar to conducting a sprint review meeting in an agile organization.

The ideal flow of information/the visualization system

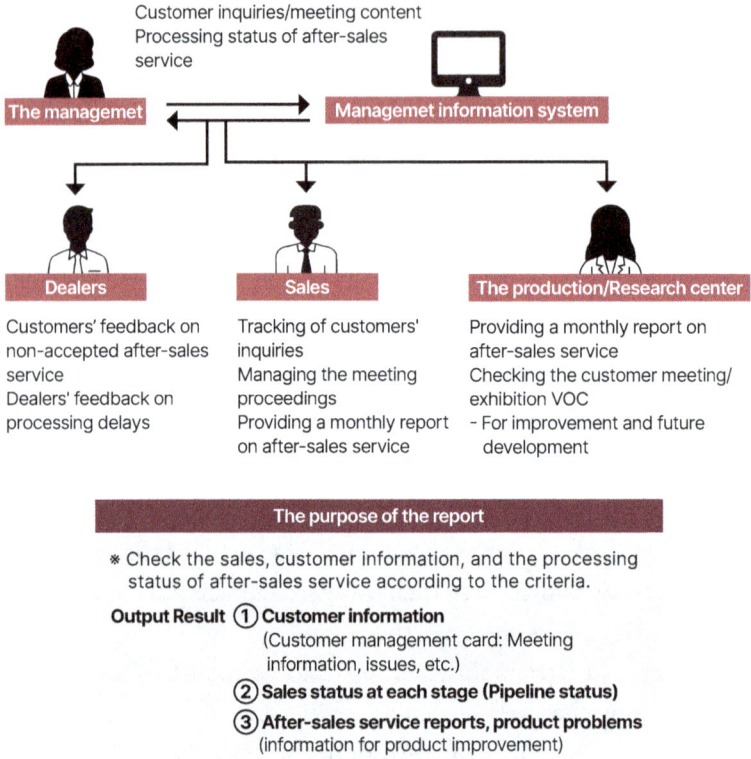

When the flow of information becomes apparent through the visualization system, all customer-related information becomes data, so the sales department can accurately deliver customers' needs and additional requirements for their products inside the organization.

Through this, the sales team will lead in information sharing for each department in the company, and provide information for issues related to product planning, marketing strategy establishment, and production response. As a result, developmental communication among departments will be possible and enabled.

Above all, since the focus is on customer decision-making, the customer-approaching strategy can be specified at each stage, according to customers' needs. In particular, for large clients, all departments will be able to intervene and respond actively, so from the sales team's perspective, they will be able to respond to customer requirements faster. Since conducting business during the COVID-19 era requires rapid responses, sales departments must accelerate their response times by helping others connect to the latest information at the center of the organization.

Reason #2 why sales departments should become insiders and information disseminators: Resolution of the silo effect

If information disconnection among departments and the departmental competition intensifies, as shown in Company A above, a profound silo effect may occur. 'Silo effect' refers to the interdepartmental egoism, in which each department only seeks internal interests without communicating with other departments, just like each department only stores fodder in its own warehouse.

A representative case of this silo effect is Sony, which was once the world's No. 1 company. Sony intentionally created silos. It created an independent checking and calculating structure for each business unit, and operated them separately. Of course, Sony did not carry out this separate management procedure from the beginning. In 1989, after founders Morita and Ibuka stepped down, Norio Ohga took over as the CEO, integrating the enormous organization and proceeding with solid, centralized governance. Sony's PlayStation was born during that time. Ohga's autocratic management style has both helped the company develop, and caused a considerable backlash. And two years later, Nobuyuki Idei took over as the new CEO, following Ohga. Unlike Ohga, Nobuyuki Idei wanted to run the company in a way that could empathize with its employees. He decided that it was necessary to subdivide the company into different professional independent groups, to manage the enormous and complex organization efficiently. Thus, Sony, which used to be a single company, was classified into eight separate companies (later reorganized into ten companies) and 25 business units. This was what Nobuyuki Idei said at that time.

"We need to simplify the organizational structure to clarify who is responsible for what, then shift and hand over the authority to respond to the external changes quickly. It is also necessary to promote entrepreneurship and reduce the hierarchy, to create a solid foundation for dynamic management to fit the 21st century."

This strategy was intended to create an independent organization and increase transparency, accountability, and efficiency, which was partly true. If an independent organization is created, each unit must be responsible for its profitability, so the organization as a whole can be more efficiently operated, and the responsibilities of the management become clearer. However, when the silo effect occurs, there must be systems or mechanisms to help overcome the shortcomings, such as information disconnection between boundaries, difficulties in collaboration, and lack of communication.

Sony had to face various problems without these systems and mechanisms. The independent business units did not exchange information with each other. They only tried to protect their department, and even began blocking the movement of excellent human resources to other business units. Of course, Nobuyuki Idei was also aware of these side effects. He emphasized the network spirit, and recommended that business units of the same product line should exchange information. However, as the internal organizational collaboration had been completely interrupted, the silo effect, in which no one wanted to communicate with each other easily, had become more serious.

When you think about it, in the late 2000s, the boundaries between the business processes of many companies began to become ambiguous. Sony's policy can be seen as reversing the trend of the times, when the destruction of business boundaries, like the boundaries between hardware and software, had intensified. We are too well aware of the results. Sony, the world's No. 1 home appliances manufacturer of products such as the Walkman and TV, has now handed over its position to Samsung Electronics.

Interestingly, Apple adopted an opposite business approach to Sony. Apple took precautions against the silo effect, and did not allow its engineers to conduct experiments individually by business unit. Jobs' successor, Tim Cook, said the following: "Apple does not have a business unit with an independent profit and loss structure. The entire company is operated with one profit and loss account."[1]

In Sony's case, the formation of silos among departments or business units blocked their eyes and ears. As a result, information exchange was cut off, and each department thought only of its own interests. In the case of Company A, which was examined above, the silo effect also occurred among different departments, and this effect has become more severe due to COVID-19.

When telecommuting and non-face-to-face communication become vital due to COVID-19, we should pay attention to the silo effect. In a non-face-to-face environment, information exchange among departments becomes tricky, so information-sharing is not carried out smoothly. In addition, other departments' situations are relatively easy to recognize and grasp face-to-face, since employees usually conduct their work in the same open space. But nowadays, employees cannot meet at the office, so the exchange of information becomes more critical. And employees are also concerned about how other people work, how they work, and what others think of them.

In such a situation where the flow of information is blocked, the sales department should be a source that facilitates its generation and flow. This is because the sales department is uniquely poised to enable both the inflow and dissemination of the information to the very front line. Therefore, the sales department should start acting as an insider rather than an outsider.

Solution #2: Integrate the strategy and execution

In the case of Company A, the strategy and product planning departments and the sales department, which is the implementation department, are operated separately. It was after the 1970s that companies began to separate their strategy and implementation departments, since they recognized the importance of strategies to cope with uncertain business environments after experiencing the oil crisis twice.[2]

Since then, each company has had departments dedicated to strategies, such as the strategic planning office and the management strategy team. The strategy departments generally set goals, profit and loss targets, and various indicators, and manage the company's resources. In other words, it plays a role in checking and managing whether the goals of the company established at the beginning of the year are being appropriately implemented, and advising on decision-making. It also plays a role in establishing a separate new business, or organizational strategy, on a macroscopic level.

In this way, an organization must establish company-wide strategies in response to new business projects. This is because a forward-looking management style, which looks at and predicts the future and prepares in advance when everyone pays attention only to the present, is essential for the organization to continue to grow. However, it is not suitable for the current COVID era to completely separate the strategy and implementation departments, and implement strategies based on processes.

Strategy implementation process

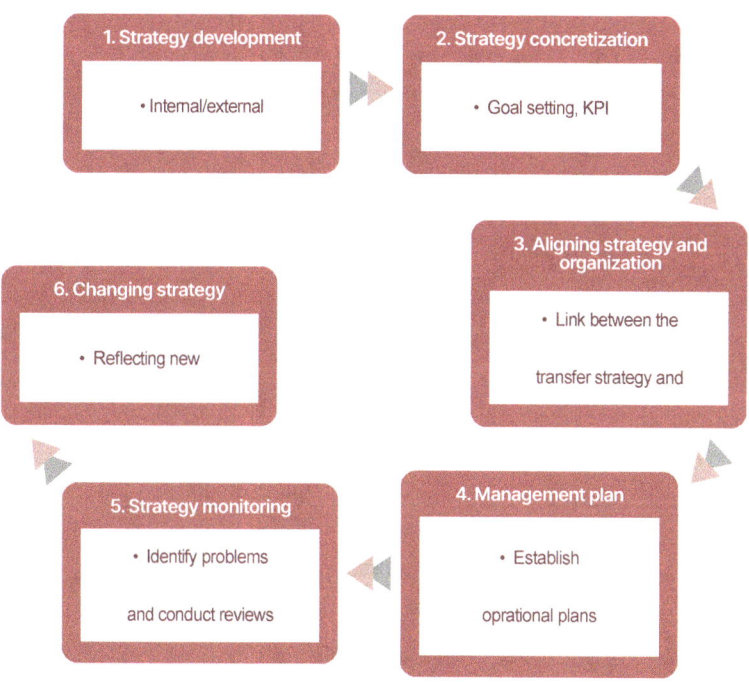

The typical strategy implementation process in companies such as Company A is as follows.

What are the problems with following this step-by-step process?

The first problem is that quick responses are restricted when new information is continuously provided. And in the case of this linear strategy execution, strategy and execution are officially separate areas, so the silo effect may arise within the above mentioned implementation and strategy departments. In particular, when establishing a strategy, the predictive power for the future is reduced, since information on the implementation stage is not obtained, eventually resulting in the incapability of quickly responding to the ever-changing customers' needs.

The second problem is that it is difficult to withdraw a strategy halfway. If the linear strategy execution method is applied, the top management or strategy establishment departments will proceed with their strategies even if they think they are wrong; they may not readily accept the reality, because they have already spent a lot of time and resources. This phenomenon is called the 'escalation of commitment,' which refers to a behavior pattern in which an individual or group is obsessed with past decisions, and decides to continue the behavior instead of altering their course—despite decisive evidence and new information appearing over time, indicating that it is a wrong choice.

In organizations, if the strategy and implementation departments are separated, it isn't easy to quickly alter the decision-making and accept this fact, even if the information is provided. As Company A's R&D department argues, it is easier to fall into the escalation of commitment as soon as they think that "planning is our responsibility, and the salespeople should focus only on implementation."

Third, the idea that we should divide the sales departments (execution/implementation departments) and the strategy departments per se falls into a kind of dogma.

In other words, it is a stereotype that the top managerial department, the management, and leadership should be in charge of establishing strategies with external strategy consultants or internal strategy departments, and other departments should focus on implementing them. Often, an organization's brain (the top management or strategy departments) engages in the thinking and decision-making process. And this brain argues that the hands and feet (execution/implementation departments) should act as the head tells them to. Many companies still manage their organizations based on this premise. For example, considering the traditional business process of the fashion industry, management and designers first lead the process by selecting the trend style expected for each season, producing it in large quantities, distributing it via each distribution channel, and selling it. The main task of frontline salespeople is to sell products made.

However, as customers' needs diversify and change rapidly, SPA brands are adopting a work process that identifies the style customers desire from frontline salespeople, quickly commercializes it, and makes the final release. The sales role is not limited to just sales but also partially to that of a product planning, value carrying, and post-purchasing manager. As in the case of Company A above, if it is necessary to respond to various customer needs and market environments actively, the integration of sales and strategies is essential. Moreover, due to COVID-19, the number of cases where salespeople must make decisions and respond quickly has increased.[3]

Amid the uncertainty of the COVID era, we have to think twice about establishing and implementing strategies. In particular, to overcome the shortcomings of the mentioned linear strategy process, and to implement strategies more flexibly, sales, strategy, and product departments must implement a loop strategy execution instead of disconnecting from each other.

Once this loop strategy execution is established, various sales information can be quickly integrated, managed, and reflected in the organizational strategies. Organizations will be able to respond promptly to changes in the external environment. In addition, since strategies and implementations are integrated, it is possible to prevent the transfer of responsibilities. As a result, rapid improvement based on continuous information-sharing is made possible.

| Loop Strategy Execution[4]

A virtuous cycle of strategy execution (Loop Strategy Execution)

1. **Collect information&Identify information patterns**[Make Sense]
   The phase to collect and analyze data to identify the diverse, complex, and incomplete patterns of information in sales
   * The phase to collect and analyze data to quickly run the Loop Strategy Execution, instead of the accurate long-term prediction

2. **Decide priorities**[Make Choices]
   The phase to clearly decide the priorities to focus on the organization's resources and interests

3. **Execute/implement the strategy**[Make Things Happen]
   The phase focuses on execution/implementation to realize the priorities mentioned above. The key here is that the goal for the entire organization must be consistent
   * Methodology available in the course of execution: Scrum, Kanban, Sprint

4. **Modify and improve the strategy**[Make Chages]
   The phase to identify new opportunities and threats, modify and improve the strategy, and prepare for re-execution. During this process, the existing method can be completely abandoned

Solution #3: Reduce the gap and strengthen the power in strategy execution

In the post-COVID era, the power of execution is significant. This is because the market changes rapidly, and quick responses are required as the business model of each competitor also changes from time to time. Previously, we looked at how to resolve the most controversial issues in Company A's case. Still, it is no exaggeration to say that the core of the problem lies in the power of execution.

Unfortunately, however, many organizations are having difficulties in execution. Reports and strategy meetings, in which plenty of time and human resources are invested to establish business strategies for the following year, take place in October every year; as a result, only plausible and pleasing documents are presented there, since they have not been implemented. Execution can be said to be the sum of daily managerial decisions. Therefore, the fundamentals of implementation are understanding the organization's decision-making structure, organizational structure, information flow and sharing, and motivating corporate members.

However, there is a tendency to only think about the organizational structure as the most crucial factor in increasing the power of execution. Of course, the organizational structure is vital. This is because the way you work and the way information flows can vary, depending on the organizational structure. Changing the organizational structure alone can have apparent effects immediately, and efficiency can be quickly enhanced. However, this is only a short-term solution—similar to, say, applying ointment because you have a pimple on your face, but not addressing the actual problem, which is that the spot may be caused by stress or unhealthy organs. Previously, Company A's problem-solving solution suggested that information sharing, the disintegration of silos, and strategy-execution integration (strategy-execution loop) could solve the root cause of the problem, instead of short-term solutions of resolving just the symptoms of the dysfunction.

▍ 4 critical elements for strengthening the power of execution

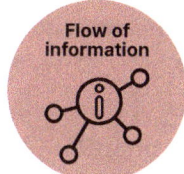

Flow of information

Is the information for strategy execution well shared within the organization?

Decision-making rights

Are strategy execution responsibilities, rights, and privileges clear and appropriately delegated?

Motivatio

Are conditions established for members to quickly implement and execute the strategies?

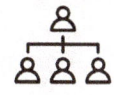

Organizational structure

Are organizational and human resources properly arranged for strategy implementation?

* The importance level of the factors is from left to right

Booz & Company surveyed to determine which of the four significant factors is the most important, to strengthen the power of execution. Among the right of decision-making, information flow, organizational structure, and motivation, the results showed that "whether decision-making rights are properly granted or whether information flow is properly carried out" were the most critical factors.[5]

The first thing many CEOs do while innovating their organizations is to integrate their business units, reduce the management departments, and take measures to strengthen their power of execution. However, changes in the organizational structure often result in a return to the previous situation when a new leader comes. This is because it only works for a short period, and does not change things fundamentally. Many companies continue to adopt various procedures to strengthen their power of execution, but they fail shortly. This is because the implementation of a strategy is not the result of a single decision or action, but an integrated chain of decisions and actions, made continuously.

After all, to enhance the organization's power of execution, information sharing for strategy execution must be prioritized. In addition, roles, responsibilities, and decision-making rights within the organization must be appropriately established. During the current COVID-19 era, more rights, privileges, and functions should be given to the sales department, and the salespeople who directly conduct sales activities.

Solution #4: Make the role of sales essential in product development as well

Previously, we saw some business process-related issues such as strategy, planning, and execution/implementation, through the example of Company A. The problems related to Company A's product development processes remain unresolved, similar to issues on the strategy implementation process. Let's look at the way Company A conducts their business again.

> When conducting organizational diagnosis for each team's issues, team leader K identified one more problem: the conflict caused by the launch of a new product. Company A planned to launch a data-based software platform in 2020, after the outbreak of COVID-19. The new platform was a system that made it easy to manage and

share hospital and patient information. Through this, Company A tried to overcome the limitations of existing medical equipment companies, and respond more actively to market changes caused by COVID-19, while maximizing the lock-in effect (customer attachment) of existing hospital customers. It was a service designed to improve the efficiency of the hospital's work, and create new values that allowed patients to access and check their information quickly.

From the company's point of view, the management's expectations and hopes were high since a lot of time, money, and even additional human resources were invested in launching the new project. Team leader K, as ever, identified the conflict between the sales and R&D departments. The sales side continued to ask the development department for customized support, because it was difficult to achieve successful outcomes unless each hospital had a 100% customized system. Since there were rumors that the competitors would launch products with similar programs within six months, the development department could not overlook the requirement of the sales department. In this case, it was not easy to secure market dominance in the future if the newly launched product failed. In particular, the business of platform launching had recently become popular among large distributors overseas, but fortunately, it had not yet become widespread in Korea; thus, product launching and early marketing were more critical. Contrary to these requirements from sales, R&D insisted that customized support, tailored toward each hospital, was impossible to ensure a flawless product launch along with the lack of human resources. Team leader K believed the sales and R&D departments' propositions all made sense. However, under the current market situation, K thought it was a priority to set a direction, and launch the product quickly to the market instead of delaying it. The problem was, 'How should an organization introduce a product that simultaneously satisfies their customers and minimizes the conflicts among different teams within the organization?'

This development process is a traditional one, also known as the waterfall model. The waterfall model is a software development technique based on the SDLC (Software Development Life Cycle), also known as "the linear sequential model, the phased life cycle."

The name was given because software (product) development is like a waterfall that keeps falling and cannot go in the opposite direction; if a process is completed, it is possible to move on to the next stage. Therefore, the characteristic of the waterfall model is that each phase of the development process is straightforward. It first analyzes the validity and the users' needs for function, performance, reliability, etc., then it designs and develops software (or hardware), then undergoes integrated tests, development completion, maintenance, and repairs.

This traditional product launching process has several problems like the strategy execution process discussed earlier. First of all, since product proposals are made first by the R&D leading research team, the product is launched only based on the ideas of a few people. It is a structure in which various ideas can be challenging to be reflected on. Second, the reflection of smooth feedback is limited. If the project is carried out phase by phase, it isn't easy to quickly apply the feedback because the work is conducted based on the functions of departments, and it also takes up plenty of time. The last problem is that there are limitations on information sharing and customer-centered product development. As it progresses phase by phase, when a problem occurs, the issue is often resolved within the department in charge of the relevant product function,

> **Company A's product launching process**
>
> Like other companies, the new product launching process proceeds in order by process function.
>
> 1. After the R&D team plans for the leading technology, the product launch begins by proposing the new product to the management and exploring its business opportunities.
>
> 2. When management accepts proposals for new products, the marketing team specifies product requirements through research on customer needs and competitors and hands them over to hardware and software teams, respectively.
>
> 3. Based on product requirements, the R&D team will determine product specifications and start product development.
>
> 4. Once the product specifications are confirmed, they will be handed over to the production team to prepare for mass production.

and information is not actively spread throughout the organization. In addition, there may be that customers' needs are not actively reflected, because products are planned and made from the perspectives of the creator or developer instead of the customers.

An organizational structure^{matrix organization} that enables the sales department to actively participate in the development and the changes in development method

Organizational structuris essential in improving traditional product development processes. There might be readers who wonder about what we said earlier, that "changing the organizational structure alone cannot be a solution." In other words, the sales, R&D, marketing, quality assurance, and production are transformed into matrix-type departments that can take action like a single team, sharing information and reflecting the customer feedback in real-time. This is to shift the existing functional organizational structure, in which the organization is divided by different functions into a matrix structure so that work can be processed on a product basis.

In this way, the sales department can more actively share information and deliver customer responses to the development department, in real-time.

| Matrix organizational structure

In terms of actual performance management, instead of simply changing the organizational structure, responsibilities, rights, and privileges can also be strengthened by simultaneously sharing the existing organizational goals and the relevant product goals, and turning these into significant indicators for performance management. In addition, it is possible to quickly develop and test products by introducing an agile methodology, instead of following traditional processes in product development. Therefore, from product development to actual sales, all departments will have a system that can share information and reflect on it. But if you're interested in agile development or management, you've probably noticed that what we've discussed so far is in line with agile management.

Sales and marketing data are collected and analyzed throughout the customer's purchasing process, to be linked to design thinking, lean startup, and agile development. In doing so, the first thing to consider should be "visualization." In the end, it is linked to the two solutions presented above, because all customer information is shared, analyzed, and reflected to improve product development, starting with customers. In the process, sales should play a leading role and, at the same time, serve as the center for producing and disseminating information.

CASE STUDY

[Spotify] Spotify's Matrix organizational structure

The matrix organizational structure and agile management were mentioned as a way to solve Company A's organizational problems. Spotify actually applied this solution. Spotify is a Swedish music streaming service company, with more than 100 million active users, and more than 30 million paid users. In 2021, it began providing services in Korea, and it is also growing by rapidly expanding its market. Since its launch in 2008, Spotify has applied an agile management methodology with self-organization teams, to continuously provide more value to their users.

The key to agile management is that it continues to pursue bottom-up innovation and customer-centered management. Spotify's team was also learning and innovating, to provide new music to customers and keep them interested. Most importantly, the company succeeded in forming an agile-based organizational culture by encouraging the members of each department to experiment and create new ways to add value to customers. Spotify's corporate members, like other development companies, succeeded because they made self-directed improvements in response to user experiences, without having to obtain approval for budget plans and proposals through a vertical organizational structure when improving and planning products. They focused on user experiences, and quickly created prototypes or conducted tests by applying alternatives, learning, and growing through them.

The basic unit of Spotify's development department is the squad. The squad is a concept similar to a scrum team, or a small organizational unit like a startup. A squad has the competency of developing a single product, from design and development to QA and product release. Since a squad is a self-organized team and determines how they work independently, some squads utilize tools like scrum and sprint, while others use kanban.

The squad encourages the application of lean startup principles such as MVP^{Minimum Viable Product}, products that can be independently executed on a minimum basis, and valid learning (a learning method that shows what is needed for growth, instead of intentionally fitting for the delivered outcome or hiding failures). MVP means launching a product frequently and quickly, and valid learning refers to the process of confirming the actual meaningful outcome generated from the A/B testing, and then improving and developing through the results.

Spotify does not appoint an official leader in the squad, but selects a product owner among product managers. Like any other agile organization, the product owners are responsible for deciding their team's priorities. Instead of controlling the squad's tasks, or interfering in each stage of the work, the role of the product owner is to be the guide and coach. The squad works like a small startup, and is guaranteed autonomy. Spotify has more than 30 squads, whose work is highly related to each other. These squads are then reorganized into higher-level groups, called "tribes." In Spotify, the tribes act as the incubator for squads. The size of a tribe does not exceed 100 people, as per 'Dunbar's Number.' Dunbar's Number suggests that 150 people are optimal for individuals to maintain stable social relationships. This theory was first proposed by Robin Dunbar, a professor at the University of Oxford. Professor Dunbar studied sociability in primates. His study found that, the larger the neocortex responsible for complex thinking, the more friends one had. It is estimated that, if this logic is applied to human beings, it will amount to about 150 people. Based on this theory, Spotify organized the tribe with less than 100 members so they could cooperate and communicate most efficiently.[6]

Of course, an organization with such maximized autonomy is not favorable in every respect. In particular, since the organization comprises small teams, its disadvantages regarding economies of scale become clear. To overcome these shortcomings, sharing knowledge and problem-solving solutions is of vital importance. For example, suppose Squad A is solving a problem already fixed last week by Squad B. In that case, the issue will be more easily resolved by information-sharing and communicating.

Spotify is overcoming these shortcomings to some extent, by forming chapters and guilds, again within the tribe. The 'chapter' refers to a group with similar areas of profession and skills within a tribe. The chapter lead is the line manager of the chapter members, and plays the role of a traditional leader in things such as member competency development and annual salary setting. However, the chapter lead is also a squad member, so they are responsible for their squad's daily work and tasks.

Furthermore, the guild is a group of people who share knowledge, tools, and insights within the organization; a more organic community. Chapters are always organized within the same tribe, but guilds are generally broadly constructed within the entire organization. For example, a web technology guild, a tester guild, a sales guild, and a marketing guild can exist in an organization. And any member interested in the guild within the organization can join it.

Spotify's organizational structure is characterized by the matrix organizational structure we discussed previously. In most organizations with a matrix organizational structure, people with similar skills are integrated into functional departments, working on a project basis and reporting to functional managers. However, Spotify does not work this way. These business units are grouped into a form in which people with different technical skills cooperate on the vertical axis, and share knowledge, tools, and code on the horizontal axis. The Project Owner (PO) plays a role in providing and managing products for customers on the vertical axis, while the chapter lead plays a role in giving mutual tension and making improvements, since they focus on creating high-quality products on the horizontal axis. Spotify focuses on delivering the final product to customers through this matrix organizational structure.[7]

One reason why we looked at Spotify's agile management is that it is an ideal agile organization. Still, it also provides hints in solving problems with organizations like Company A. Since it is a software development organization, hardware-based manufacturers will not be able to work 100% in the same way.

However, suppose the information that a sales or marketing department obtains from customers can be quickly reflected in product development and improvements. In that case, this system can be an ideal blueprint for organizational operations in the COVID era.

Let's reconsider the case of Company A. The requirements that Team Leader K received from the management were to change how the sales department worked, and resolve conflicts among various departments. However, the problem could be solved only by applying an agile methodology to the entire company. Agile management is never about advanced technology or skills, but attitudes, such as customer-centered thinking, smooth information delivery, collaboration based on a horizontal organizational culture, an open-ended culture and strategies, and customer feedback to improve products.

However, even if the transition to agile organization and management takes place, the company cannot succeed unless the organizational culture changes. The essential growth components for agile organizations are a collaboration among teams, delegating authority and trust at the product level instead of centralized control, strengthening networks by function, and adjusting relationships among groups. In the end, what's important is the organizational culture and mind.[8]

Shifting the way you work to agile is also a leadership issue. As mentioned earlier, an agile organization works around customers, and quickly reflects feedback for revision and improvement, so there is bound to be a lot of information and changes. In this situation, a mistake often made by leaders is an attempt to increase control. They want more reporting, more involvement in decisions, and sometimes want to enhance the power of a functional organizational structure.

A functional organizational structure with centralized control can be hazardous in an agile organization. Suppose you want to work centered around the customers. In that case, quick responses are essential, because decision-making can be slowed down, and flexibility can be hindered due to an excess in control. It is necessary to find an appropriate balance of trust and authority, systematically change it, and simultaneously create a business environment that enables growth through failure and learning, which is the core of agile culture.

Lastly, the core of this case is "how to define and apply the agile method of marketing and sales." In the context of sales and marketing, agile means analyzing the data collected from various channels to find solutions to problems in real-time, applying them to online/offline channels from an IMC perspective, testing them, evaluating results, and repeating all these processes quickly. It should also play a role in rapidly disseminating this kind of information to the development team.

Introduction of agile-related terminologies for sales leaders

- **Lean Startup**
  Lean Startup is a business strategy that quickly transforms ideas into minimal functional products (prototypes), then examines market reactions to improve and develop products. In particular, Lean Startup, like other agile methodologies, prioritizes customers, applies fast learning methods, and values feedback. Lean Manufacturing, which Toyota first started, is the predecessor of Lean Startup. The key to lean manufacturing is to draw out the knowledge and creativity of individual workers, reduce the number of products produced at a time, manage production and inventory promptly, and quickly turn this cycle around. Lean Startup applied these ideas to the entrepreneurial spirit. The core of Lean Startup is to create and evaluate MVP (Minimum Viable Product), a product with just enough features to be used for experiments. For example, if the goal of the final product is a finished car, a prototype that meets the minimum need for transportation is created and tested.

- **Design thinking**

First introduced in the 1990s by design consulting firm IDEO, design thinking is critical in identifying key customer needs based on customer-centric thinking to create products or services. After identifying key customer needs, a series of solutions should be proposed to meet customer needs and be technically feasible and suitable for the business through brainstorming.

- **Scrum**
Scrum is the oldest and most well-known methodology of agile development and is characterized by developing in short sprint units (short units that produce products, repetitive development cycles). The focus is on minimizing the complexity of software development and providing products and services tailored to customer needs. It is also characterized by holding daily stand-up meetings and retrospectives (feedback) for continuous improvement and development to deliver products tailored to customer needs. In scrum, the development team is self-organized. Here, being self-organized means each team member decides their work based on autonomy and responsibility instead of a traditional vertical and bureaucratic organizational structure of working under someone's instructions.

- **Kanban**
Kanban means a bulletin board in Japanese, which refers to a system for timely production. This is said to have been applied to automobile production plants when the executives of Toyota got the idea by looking at the cards used on supermarket shelves when they visited the United States. The core of Kanban is to efficiently manage inventory by producing only as many products as customers want and promptly providing parts for the following process. Kanban focuses on more elastic alternatives, predictable results, transparency, and delivery of the developed products. In addition, development progress can be transparently shared

with customers. When customers share Kanban, real-time feedback, transparent result sharing, and a customer-centered approach, which is the agile principle, can be proceeded more clearly.

- **XP (Extreme Programming)**
  XP is a software development methodology that improves software quality and responsiveness to changing customer requirements. As an agile methodology, XP supports more frequent releases with shorter development cycles for end users. The name XPExtreme Programming comes from the idea to immensely and exceedingly develop the software engineering competency within the team. In XP, it is assumed that it can boost the competencies by promoting continuous code reviews via pair programming. Here, pair programming means pairing the program development together.

- **DevOps**
  DevOps is one of the most used and mentioned agile methodologies in recent years. DevOps aims to integrate agile infrastructure into the software development process, and the key is to enable rapid release by uniting the development and operations teams. To this end, collaboration and communication are among the most important critical issues, and the culture allows for such cooperation instead of technology.

The 'Agile Management' that sales leaders should consider in the New Normal era

▌ This chapter summarizes the roles that sales departments should play in strategy execution and product development in the COVID-19 era, and the directions that should be shifted from the perspective of organizational operations. And we find that many parts align with agile management by putting together the things we looked at earlier. Overall, what sales leaders and managers should consider now is understanding agile management's philosophy and background. In particular, many leaders often regard agile as only a methodology for development, and focus only on working fast. But, in fact, agile is directly related to leadership, culture, and way of working.

The background and basic principles of Agile Management

To understand agile management, it is first necessary to understand the core value of the Manifesto for Agile Software Development. The Agile Manifesto contains the philosophy of a new agile approach, not the existing method, and includes 12 principles that support it.

Understanding the principles and philosophy of this manifesto is imperative to change the current way of working, and apply a new development methodology. Many organizations and IT development companies seek innovation but fail to use it properly, because they do not understand the background, philosophy, and culture contained in the Agile Manifesto. Since most organizations focus only on agile tools and processes per se, and are not very interested in the way or principles of work, they often fail to introduce the methodology. Particularly for many Korean companies, managers tend to be sensitive to trends in organizational operations. Therefore, if any advanced company overseas has success using agile methodology, the tool or process is often unconditionally introduced, instructed, and applied. Companies that request consulting or training on agile methodology are often obsessed with its tools and systems, focusing on flexibility and quick responses, which are only a tiny part of it, instead of its culture or philosophy. In the case of such companies, it is evident that the agile methodology will spread like a trend for a while, eventually fizzle out, and then the company will return to its original state. What matters is agile culture and philosophy. You have to understand why agile was born, what direction it pursues, and the critical values of agile.

The Agile Manifesto can be said to be the source of agile tools and principles. Therefore, for companies that want to introduce this methodology, the Agile Manifesto can serve as a guideline. Looking at it, you can tell the attitude of innovation is to alter the paradigm of traditional development methodologies and to focus on a human-centered and value-oriented approach, where agile is not just about tools or processes but the desire for change in mindset and value structure.

> **Manifesto for Agile software development**[9]
>
> **We are uncovering better ways to develop software by doing it and helping others do it. Through this work we have come to value:**
>
> 1. Individuals and interactions over processes and tools
>
> 2. Working software over comprehensive documentation
>
> 3. Customer collaboration over contract negotiation
>
> 4. Responding to change over following a plan
>
> That is, while there is value in the items on the right side of each sentence, we value the items on the left more.

1. Value individuals and interactions over processes and tools.

In the case of the traditional development methodology we have looked at earlier, the process and integrality of each step are essential. In particular, many organizations only emphasize efficiency and productivity based on Taylorism (the principles of scientific management and work efficiency), and their members are often regarded simply as tools or components of a process. However, agile methodology values people and development through relationships and interactions. No matter how perfect the system or tool is, it does not work out correctly if the people who use it encounter problems, or if communication and relationships among various departments or teams are not effective and smooth. After all, work proceeds, and results are achieved through interrelationships among organizational members.

2. Value working software over comprehensive documentation·

The key here is to focus on practicality instead of formalism. Suppose you focus too much on formalism and fail to invest the necessary time in practice, in order to improve performance. You are putting the cart before the horse. The Agile Manifesto advocates the value of avoiding unnecessaries, and focusing on the core to increase efficiency.

3. Value customer collaboration over contract negotiation.

Agile is thoroughly customer-centered. It aims to listen to customers' voices and quickly reflect them in the company's products and strategy. Therefore, it is inevitably sensitive to the market response, and customer-related information must be rapidly spread within the organization.

4. Value responding to change over following a plan.

In the past, responding to changes in a business environment was challenging, because compliance with processes and plans was necessary. After the project was over, new plans were often established and responded to. Of course, complying with procedures and schedules in a business environment where specific patterns were predictable, was vital. However, in today's business environment, especially in the era of VUCA, where consumer needs change frequently and rapidly, if you proceed with the project as planned, you may miss opportunities, and your business may encounter difficulties. Therefore, the development methodology that responds appropriately to changes and constantly makes improvements will be more suitable for today's situation. The Agile Manifesto places more value on responding flexibly to changes.

To summarize the agile principles and values mentioned above, agile seeks to provide continuous customer value based on customer-centric thinking, and puts more weight on people than on vertical organizational structure or processes. Because of this flexible approach, many startups are cultivating an agile culture, becoming the subject of innovation. However, other companies also have many things to refer to and apply to their organizations from the agile philosophy and values, such as the application of the customer-centric working methods from an organization's point of view, recruitment (the point of view regarding a talent when hiring), talent development, motivation, and employee participation, as well as evaluation and compensation.

Traditional management vs. Agile management

Despite the need for a more flexible approach to cope with the rapidly changing business environment in the VUCA era, many organizations still cannot abandon their existing way of working with a production manufacturing-based mindset, which is a typical Taylorism. The top-down and bureaucratic working method, which has been applied in the existing labor-intensive industry, is no longer efficient. This is why more and more companies are taking a strategic approach that can be used more flexibly to suit each organization's situation, or the situation of a specific region, instead of making decisions at the control tower, governing, and giving command from the top.

In this regard, it is clear that we should start by applying agile principles. Though the agile principles began with software development, they provide an opportunity to work more efficiently throughout the company, and flexibly respond to the changing business environment. When we apply the agile methodology to

Contrast and comparison between traditional and agile management[10]

Category	Traditional management	Agile management
Process	• Short, Phased • Standardized • Linear response • One-sided (Push)	• Continuous development based on learning • Based on customer needs • Reaction loop (a virtuous cycle) • Interactive (Pull)
Organization	Vertical	Horizontal (Network)
Leadership	Management	Delegation of authority
Point of view regarding people	Theory X (Negative, control is needed)	Theory Y (Positive, autonomy over control)
Motivation	Extrinsic motivation (e.g., monetary compensation)	Intrinsic motivation (e.g., vision, autonomy)
Feedback	Proceed passively at a settled time	Periodically and actively

the existing status quo, the key is processes, organizations, leadership, point of view regarding people, motivation, and feedback.

Let's look at the differences between the existing way of working, and the way of working based on agile principles. First, in terms of processes, if the current methodology proceeds step by step according to the settled process, the agile methodology usually experiences failures quickly—and learns from them to achieve continuous development. In addition, if the existing methods respond to requirements, the agile methodology makes suggestions beforehand according to the situation, and responds efficiently to the customers' needs. In terms of organizations, the traditional method prefers vertical decision-making with a top-down approach. The agile methodology encourages communication through a more horizontal organizational structure. Above all, the biggest difference between leadership and point of view is when it comes to people. According to the traditional methodology, people are viewed as objects to be controlled and managed, based on Theory X. The agile method is based on Theory Y, where autonomy and trust are highly valued. In addition, there is a big difference in feedback. The traditional work is carried out without feedback until a certain point. However, the agile methodology learns, improves, and develops through periodic feedback. We have previously discussed the points that need to change in how sales teams work and interact with leadership, and we can tell that many facets are intricately interlinked.

The misunderstanding of "horizontal leadership"

When talking about agile and horizontal organizational structure, many leaders think that autonomous management is helpful for corporate operations. Still, they feel uncertain. If the organization is left with too much autonomy, wouldn't it be difficult to operate? However, autonomy does not mean making concessions to organizational members and letting them do whatever they want. In other words, the core of agile management is to work based on results and customers, so it requires much concentration, and must accept the market's ruthless assessment. The following is a meeting between a team leader and a team member of a company.

> **The Team Leader** Shall we look at the market research data I mentioned last time? The proposal will be submitted next week, so I hope we can do an interim review.
> **Assistant Manager A** Um, I'm still working on it… Let me show you first.
> **The Team Leader** Hmm… I think it's a little insufficient; why don't

we also include how our customer's competitors are doing? Wouldn't the customers be curious about that?

Assistant Manager A Since you granted me the authority for this project, can't you just wait and see? I don't know if it makes sense for me to continue with this project if I have to follow your plan.

The Team Leader (very flustered) A, giving you feedback does not mean that you didn't do well; it's because I want you to do better, to reflect the customer's point of view, so don't feel too offended. Revise it as I said, and let's discuss it tomorrow.

Assistant Manager A ...Okay.

Backstage...

Assistant Manager A This is so annoying. They say autonomy, horizontal culture... If they order me around like this, the leader should have done it from the beginning.

Manager B What's wrong?

Assistant Manager A Isn't our company an organization that pursues working autonomy and a horizontal structure? If they're going to give directions and control me like this, I don't know why they're emphasizing an agile culture.

Manager B If you are a team member, you must do what they say. Agile? Forget it. They're just saying that.

Perhaps this is what most leaders find challenging these days. Sharing opinions horizontally and freely is the culture that agile management aims for. However, a horizontal organization does not mean operations without a vertical command system. Moreover, agile management should instead communicate based on results. If there is a problem, agile management prevails to resolve it without making concessions. When discussing a horizontal organizational culture, we should be careful that granting autonomy does not mean indulging. It's not just allowing people to do whatever they want. Of course, it does not mean coercive control either. Both leaders and organizational members need to work autonomously, but must be strict about their work, not compromise on performance, and pursue customer-centric results (customer satisfaction). As a result, if agile management (culture) was adequately approached in the above case, we should have been able to observe an attitude to thrive for a better solution, without making any concession over the proposal output (for customer delivery).

Then there will be leaders who ask questions like this: "Well, what can I do when employees only emphasize autonomy and a horizontal culture, and end up not listening to me?" This may not only be the leaders' fault. The entire organization must work together. Agile management pursues autonomy, but decisive leadership and interference also follow. Agile management is a methodology for all organizational members to produce the best outcome, and respond quickly to customer feedback. However, it may be difficult for members with little experience or know-how to deliver the optimal result; thus, leaders who support their members are needed. Without leader interference, all organizational members must have a considerable level of professionalism (in terms of work and attitude). Therefore, this must be emphasized and considered when hiring and cultivating members. In reality, because Netflix and Google aim for such an autonomous and agile culture, they hire people with a stricter standard, with the image of talent that the organization wants, and resolutely weed out those who do not meet the criteria.

Many companies, including Netflix, strive to hire the best talent, so they can have opportunities to grow together with their employees and achieve the most optimized results. Behind this logic, however, a framework of responsibilities, requirements to be qualified as a good colleague, decisive leadership, and followership are in action. That's why we shouldn't just focus on things that sound magnificent, such as autonomy and a horizontal organizational structure, when we look at and talk about agile.

Agile culture, and culture of the MZ[Millennials] and Gen Z generation

Since 2018, each company has been scrambling to learn Agile. In particular, plenty of education related to agile leadership came out for organizational leaders. People are becoming more interested in agile as the agile methodology, which quickly releases the products to the market, and tests the products, has become popular, especially among startups.

Earlier, we pointed out the misunderstandings of autonomy and indulgence of agile management; still, there is one more thing to consider. Among the characteristics of agile management, it is thought that agile management focuses only on rapidly testing the market and improving the product through failures; it is believed that agile is only about quick responses. Agile does mean moving quickly, but you should not be obsessed with that specific wording. Instead, more attention should be paid to the trend of the times and social changes. Among them, we would like to say that the "MZ generation's characteristics and the culture that follows" are very similar to the agile culture. We should pay attention to agile management and culture in the COVID-19 era, because these methods are suitable for creating a horizontal organizational culture in a non-face-to-face environment. In addition, agile culture is closely related to the values pursued by the MZ generation.

In February 2021, it became a major social issue in Korea when organizational members of SK Hynix complained about their performance-based compensation. Employees strongly objected to the announcement that 400% of the basic salary would be paid as a bonus based on management performance in 2020. In particular, it became a hot topic that assistant manager-level employees directly sent emails to all the employees, including the CEO, raising objections to the unfairness of the performance-based compensation system. SK Hynix employees said the significant gap with Samsung Electronics' semiconductor employees, who receive 47% of their annual salary as their performance-based compensation, was "unintelligible."

These SK-initiated issues related to performance-based compensation even affected employees of other companies, such as Samsung and LG. Samsung Electronics VD division employees received 50% OPI (Overall Performance Incentive), while CE home appliance division employees received 37%, sparking controversy over equity. In the past, there was an implicit rule that even if it was unfair and resentful, it was decided by the company, so it should be followed. But these days, the MZ generation thinks these issues cannot be overlooked.[11]

Opinions are different within the companies, over the issue that the MZ generation cannot accept such a situation. On one hand, there is an opinion saying, "These days, employees are very fearless. I can't understand why they have protested like that on something set by the company. Can't they just do better next time and earn it?" On the other hand, there are also people saying, "I feel relieved. It is fortunate to see them speaking up about the things we weren't able to, and looking out for the interests of employees." However, this issue is too severe to be overlooked. "Young people these days are so bold!" We must consider the MZ generation's way of thinking and communication here.

Lim Heung-taek, the author of People Born in the 90s Are Coming, says honesty is the representative character trait of that generation. One of the values they consider vital are transparency and honesty. They are characterized by a longing for honesty, both in themselves and in others. For example, if the company that hired them, or the company whose products they use is not honest or ethical, they do not accept it, and respond accordingly.

Chung Tae-young, CEO of Hyundai Card, who pursues a unique and horizontal organizational culture, said in an interview, "If CEOs want to let their words reach the bottom of the company, they should always keep their word. If they said, 'You can use your vacation as you want,' there should be no problem whenever their employees want to go on vacation, and if they told the employees, 'You can smoke in front of me,' it should be okay to smoke together during a meeting. Trust in a company is to not even tell a small lie."[12]

In other words, extreme honesty and transparency are the attitudes that leaders should possess now. After all, the issue of performance-based compensation was triggered by the organizations' methods of handling it, and the fact that they were not transparent. Honesty and transparency are also the core values pursued by agile management. And in the era of COVID-19, when non-face-to-face situations are increasing, trust between leaders and organizational members becomes possible only when this transparency and honesty are supported.

CHECKLIST

Post-COVID era, organizational operations, and agile management diagnosis table

Category	Checklist
Visualization of information (Visualization of sales)	☐ Is information such as customers, markets, and competitors well communicated throughout the organization?
	☐ Is various information directly collected by salespeople visualized within the organization's system? * Visualization of sales: all information generated from business activities are transparently exposed, tacit knowledge (sales know-how, information) is managed as DB (data), and explicit knowledge.
	☐ Does the sales department serve as a connection and collaborate with the development, marketing, and strategy departments?
Strategy and execution	☐ Are the strategy, development (product planning), and execution departments integrated, and are the strategies implemented quickly?
	☐ Is the strategy execution taking place in an execution loop (a virtuous cycle) instead of a linear process, and is the feedback rapidly reflected in the strategy?
	☐ Are strategies implemented considering the four major factors to enhance the power of strategy execution? * The four major factors : information flow, decision-making rights, motivation, and organizational structure
	☐ Are products being developed with an organizational structure (matrix organizational structure) capable of an agile approach?
Agile Management	☐ Does our organization focus on customer-centric problem-solving instead of processes and formalism?
	☐ Does our organization focus on actively responding to changes instead of simply following plans?
	☐ Do our organizational leaders understand the genuine meaning of horizontal leadership? (To ensure that corporate members can freely discuss and present their opinions to achieve the best outcome)
	☐ Is our organization operated based on extreme honesty and transparency?

Chapter 6

Sales New Normal #6

Let's start for change

In the New Normal era, Requirements for change in the sales departments

So far, we have looked at changes in roles and competencies that sales departments, and leaders need in the post-COVID-19 era. The important thing is practice. But, that is also the most challenging thing. Moreover, the sales department is among the most difficult ones to change, since it has a strict vertical hierarchy. However, as we have seen so far, changes for survival are essential in the post-COVID-19 era.

Then, let's look at what desirable organizational culture the sales departments should pursue, and how leaders should lead it.

CASE STORY 6

A sales department's operations and transition

* The story is based on an actual case, and some details/information have been changed.

The following is a meeting of the sales department of fashion company X. Company X holds a weekly sales performance meeting, with the director of the sales department, team leaders, and division leaders. Most sessions are led by the director of the sales department and some team leaders.

The Director Although it is difficult due to COVID-19, thanks to the newly introduced live commerce and online malls, sales are still similar to the previous year. But, at times like this, we need to keep our eyes open. By the way, how are you doing these days, coming to the office 3 days a week and spending the rest of your time working from home?
All members ...
The Director Are there any issues?

Team Leader 1 first speaks up, after hesitating.
Team Leader 1 We couldn't get used to it, at first, but now everyone is satisfied with the time management in many aspects.
The Director Of course, the team leaders would be satisfied. You don't have to see me every day! Isn't that so? What about other team members?
All members ...
The Director (Sigh) Why aren't you talking? Aren't we a horizontal organization? We can't improve the system if you don't speak up. Well, by the way, it seems that the sales information and data input are not working well on the newly introduced system; even if the majority of the work is conducted online, the record of agencies, problems, and issues must be well recorded, so that we can continue to manage them post-COVID—though it's not easy. Is there anything else you have to say? If there isn't, let's wrap up here. Keep up the excellent work.

Company X is undergoing many changes due to COVID-19. It is responding to the changing market by rapidly shifting its business model, such as launching online businesses. In addition to its business transformation, there are many changes in how they work, including introducing a new information-sharing system.

Although the company has been making some achievements thanks to its active response to changes at the organizational level, the director of the sales department is frustrated that the pace of change is slow, and the corporate members do not follow the changes so well. The director of the sales department recognizes two main problems. First, members are not actively pursuing the newly introduced system. As seen from the meeting situation, communication is not smooth, and accordingly, information collected is not well disseminated. How would you resolve this issue if you were the director of Company X's sales department?

Organizations resist change by nature

Anyone who has worked for a long time, may have seen many cases where an organization tried to change their system by introducing a new one, and the attempt failed in less than a year or two. Dr. Edward Miller, who served as dean of The Johns Hopkins University School of Medicine and chief executive officer of Johns Hopkins Medicine, tells us how difficult it is to change, based on his experiences. According to him, it was observed that 90% of patients who underwent coronary artery bypass surgery due to heart problems, did not change their lifestyles even two years after the surgery.[1]

Even though one's life is at stake, changing existing habits or behaviors is difficult. Therefore, it makes sense that it is not easy to induce changes in organizational members. Refusing to change is rooted in human instinct. Suppose you do something different than before, following someone else's instructions instead of your own choices; you will feel that your freedom as a human is constrained, causing a psychological response called Reactance. This is the "Theory of Psychological Reactance."[2]

This resistance appears when you feel that your freedom is lost or threatened. The reactance is more substantial when asked to do something, than when asked not to do something. For example, suppose that a new business guideline has been created that all participants must speak at the meeting. Even those who actively spoke up during the meetings in the past, would inevitably develop a sense of resistance. They would perceive it as participation by guidelines, not by their own will. They would think they should do it because the policies were set, but on the contrary, they would end up not following this particular rule. In this way, humans naturally operate their defensive systems against external attacks.

Therefore, as in the case of Company X introduced above, it is natural for the human defensive mechanism to work against new changes. Moreover, this rejection and resistance are apparent, because the sales departments are operated more by following the existing rules instead of changing them. Therefore, leaders who try to initiate change should stop panicking about the corporate members who resist change. It is a natural phenomenon, and requires a step-by-step approach.

First, it is necessary to involve the organizational members from the planning stage. If the members plan their change direction and directly design the step-by-step action plan, the resistance can be significantly reduced. Following a procedure unilaterally, and directly developing the change direction is entirely different. In the latter case, since they think they are leading the change, the changing process can be more actively facilitated and promoted. Company X should also pay more attention in this regard. Suppose the sales system had to be changed due to COVID. In that case, it should not just have the sales department design the system at the organizational level and force the members to follow, but rather have members feel the need to change the system themselves, and participate in the designing of it, even by just a little.

Second, it is necessary to break down the Cognitive Dissonance. Cognitive dissonance refers to a state in which one's attitude and behavior are inconsistent and contradictory, often occurring when an organization pushes for change.

The Thai Health Promotion Foundation conducted a campaign to reduce the smoking rate, which had the children ask adults who were smoking if they could borrow cigarettes. Of course, Thai smokers reacted, "I can't give a cigarette to you," and "If you smoke, you will get esophageal cancer. Surgery is scary, isn't it?" mostly informing and warning the children of the dangers of cigarettes. Interestingly, they continued to smoke, even though they were already aware of the dangers and health hazards of smoking. Didn't what they said to the children also apply to themselves?

In the video, the children were rejected or even scolded for asking for cigarettes, but did not leave, and instead handed the smokers a piece of paper. The paper said this: "You were worried about me. But why aren't you worried about yourself?" And a phone number was also written on the note, to help them quit smoking.[3]

The campaign was conducted in Thailand under the name "Smoking Kid." Almost all adults whom the children had handed notes to, decided to quit smoking. If we put a sales team into a similar context, any salesperson would want to achieve higher and perform better. To deliver results in changing situations, one's sales approaches and methods must also change. But in reality, how should they go about it? Corporate members are often unaware that their methods are different from the effective ways to generate optimized results, or think the direction of such change is irrelevant to them. Therefore, communication and periodic feedback must be provided so members can recognize the difference between the actual direction of change (after COVID-19, changes in the way sales work, and the system) and how they work. Only when they recognize that they are the subject of change can they let go of the attitude that change has nothing to do with them, as if they are mere spectators.

Third, leaders should play the role of helpers. U.S. Army General George Smith Patton Jr left this quote: "Don't tell people how to do things; tell them what to do and let them surprise you with their results."[4]

As discussed in this book, leaders should be active helpers instead of controllers or dictators when bringing about change. In other words, they should be the catalyst. It does not mean that leaders should not interfere, but they should be active supporters so members can push for change. And it is necessary to continuously communicate about the direction, goal, and vision of change. Change can never happen, or last, unless the leaders closely pay attention to it and manage the transition. For Company X's transformation to be successful, the director of the sales department and the team leaders must continue to play the role of helpers, and support their members.

So far, we have seen why change is difficult, and what is essential for change. Now, let's look at how to solve Company X's organizational issues in earnest.

"Silence is golden(?)" Team members who do not speak up

We have understood the resistance to change, and considered the essential elements for making change happen. Then, what should we do with employees who don't speak up?

Earlier, we mentioned that some members did not actively participate in the meetings. The leader led the discussion, and only some members participated. In reality, most companies will not be different from Company X's situation. What is your organization like? Isn't there an organizational culture where members tend to keep silent? We already know that communication and a horizontal corporate culture in non-face-to-face environments, such as telecommuting, are crucial in the post-COVID-19 era. Then, what kind of culture should sales leaders cultivate?

Let's go back to the meeting scene of Company X. In the workplace, most of the members will be silent, like the members of Company X. They want to hide their opinions, themselves, personalities, etc., and stay quiet. This phenomenon is called "covering" in psychology. It is a phenomenon in which one hides one's personality, values, and opinions to avoid conflicts. We are putting plenty of energy into hiding ourselves.[5]

As we avoid conflicts within or between teams, we act passively even when we have to develop new ideas and opinions, and actively communicate. Everyone wants to be seen as intelligent, capable, and helpful to others. Perhaps even since elementary school, we have considered what others think of ourselves as of vital importance. From then on, we started to pick up how to reduce the risk of rejection or disregard by the other party. And when we become adults, we get used to these methods.

A TV program once tested what would happen when a student asked questions in class, at a university. The production team required one student to ask five questions during the same lecture, and looked at other students' responses in the classroom; other students began to stare at the second question. The interviews with the students after class were even more shocking. Regarding the student who asked the questions, there were opinions such as "Showing off?" and "I thought it was strange because, usually, no one asks questions." Regarding the reason for not asking, there were answers such as "I've been scolded for asking useless questions in class, so I haven't been asking questions since."

Readers reading this may have similar experiences. Perhaps we have grown up accustomed to silence. In a way, maybe we're too familiar with these phenomena and attitudes. Corporate members whom this attitude has tamed since childhood are thoroughly hiding themselves, even at work.[6]

- If I don't want to look ignorant? ⇨ Then don't ask questions.
- If I don't want to look incompetent? ⇨ Then don't admit to any mistakes or weaknesses.
- If I don't want to be stigmatized as someone who makes trouble at work? ⇨ Then don't talk at all during the meeting.

These attitudes will only make you a mediocre employee during meetings. The problem is that mediocrity does not help individuals, teams, or organizations. Thus, a culture should be cultivated where members can actively express their opinions and share information transparently. This means that a sense of psychological safety must be established within the organization. Psychological safety refers to an organizational environment in which members strongly believe they will not be punished or retaliated for any opinion regarding their work.[7] Leaders should make more efforts to create a sense of psychological safety because the culture of not speaking up is already deeply ingrained in Korean organizations.

In 2015, Google's "Project Aristotle" found that this psychological safety was the most critical factor for success in becoming high-performance teams across the organization. In particular, it was also found that individual team members' abilities were less important than the team's way of working (the way team members share information and collaborate). In addition, team members were more likely to take initiatives to share new information or take on challenges when other members did not criticize them, and their interrelationships were not damaged even if they made mistakes when coming up with an idea.

According to a 2017 survey conducted in Australia on psychological safety in the workplace, only 24% gave a positive answer. This survey was based on various factors such as gender, income, age, and educational background, and the results were as follows. First, young employees showed deeper concerns about mistakes at work (36% among young employees compared to 12-21% among manager-level employees) and relatively low psychological safety. 24% of young employees said it was difficult to ask their colleagues for help (overall average 18%). Also, when members were highly educated, they were more likely to feel psychological safety (40%) than employees with lower educational backgrounds (25%).[8]

In the case of Company X, relatively lower-level employees and young salespeople were reluctant to speak up, because it was somewhat difficult for them to feel a sense of psychological safety—and they were familiar with the culture of being silent, just as the survey results. Is your organization promoting psychological safety? Or, does your organization assume that "Our employees don't usually give opinions!" and move on as if nothing has happened? And thus, problems are overlooked? Or, perhaps, are they encouraging a culture of staying silent? It is difficult to communicate face-to-face with each other during the COVID era; the possibility of members being psychologically insecure will inevitably increase. This is why leaders should now pay more attention to psychological safety. And silent organizations and members should no longer be overlooked.

A culture of sharing information and accepting failures

After the outbreak of COVID-19 in January 2020, Korea was one of the countries in the world that was able to respond to the changing environment best. The media analyzed the successful reasons for K-quarantine every day. Among them, the New York Times cited three reasons South Korea successfully overcame the pandemic, in an article titled "How South Korea Flattened the Curve" on March 23, 2020. The answer is: through learning, tracking, and information sharing.[9]

Korea had already experienced MERS Middle East Respiratory Syndrome in 2015. At that time, Korea initially failed to respond, with 38 people dying as a result, and the fatality rate reaching as high as 14%. Due to the nature of the virus, which had an incubation period of two to fourteen days, we already knew that even if a specific area is closed after the outbreak, the spread cannot be prevented without controlling those close contacts. These experiences were not just experiences, but remained as various data and records, and were used as reference materials for our preemptive responses to COVID-19. It became good learning material.

The second is tracking. The Korean government, which experienced the importance of tracking and monitoring contacts based on the previous case, could track all the infected and contacts from scratch. Korea had already established a system to track down contacts during MERS. Tracking methods such as video surveillance (CCTV), credit card information, and mobile phone GPS were integrated and analyzed, effectively preventing the spread of infectious diseases.

The last one is information-sharing. Korea has actively opened all information to the public. Unlike China's policies of information control, Korea's information was transparently available to the public; based on this, the entire nation could respond effectively. KDCA^(Korea Disease Control and Prevention Agency) broadcasted news twice a day, and provided information on real-time confirmed cases in each region.

The success stories mentioned above are reminiscent of the sales departments' sales processes. Sales departments must transparently share all the information they have, and analyze and respond to issues or information related to the past. In the case of Company X, a sales management system was introduced after COVID-19 to enable the information to be shared more efficiently. In the past, it used to be a system managed by individual employees. However, after the pandemic, this new system was established, since the management believed that sharing information more transparently would increase efficiency and speed up decision-making.

The problem was that members did not actively follow the introduction of the system, or the procedural changes, as mentioned previously by the director of the sales department. Salespeople had to unreservedly share the tacit knowledge and customer data that only they had access to, which could cause them to bear some weight. The following was part of an interview with the director of Company X's sales department. We were able to identify the hardships he felt in the process of pursuing change.

Q. What was the most challenging thing when adopting changes after COVID-19?

The Director   My biggest challenge was that organizational members thought they were being micro-managed by us introducing the new system, and felt reluctant to change. I totally understand their feelings. They might feel uncomfortable opening up their work and reviewing the process. Furthermore, since trust has not been established within our organization, they must have regarded it as difficult, and have been experiencing hardships.

Q. It must have been challenging to disclose information transparently.

The Director   Yes. Changing the system and how you work is related to the organizational culture. Unfortunately, our corporate culture is stingy with failure. As a result, the sales team is afraid of failing, so they hesitate to try; even if the sales proceed competently, they only talk about it if a purchase is confirmed. That's why our team tried to encourage failures and information-sharing, so that we wouldn't be afraid of failing, instead turning it into an opportunity where we can learn from each other.

Q. What did you do first to solve these problems?

The Director   The communication has been exceedingly effective. I tried to explain the legitimacy of the new way of working and its values. We discussed the advantages of developing the competencies, sharing information via the system to reduce duplicate sales orders, and making it easy for salespeople who transfer to another sales region to access information and data. I also emphasized that their experiences or failures were considered assets for our organization; they would not be criticized or rebuked, even if they shared their unsuccessful experiences. Unsuccessful experiences here indicate attempting to propose to prospective customers but failing to sell. Of course, there were also cases where the marketing process performed worse than expected. But all of this information became valuable assets for us. When the experiences are built up, and information is shared, we can make improvements and increase the rate of our sales success the next time similar cases occur.

In conclusion, as seen in the interview, employees can accept change only when an organizational culture of psychological safety and accepting failures is pre-established. In addition, it should be noted that the sales department director made every effort to actively communicate and explain the importance and legitimacy of these changes. Earlier, it was mentioned that minimizing resistance to change was the role of the leaders, and Company X's sales department and its director did their best to do so. After all, changes should begin with the leaders.

Collective/group intelligence over groupthink

Sales leaders should create a culture in which they listen to various opinions of their team members, and enable accessible communication to prevent group thinking and cultivate collective intelligence. Group thinking is a concept proposed by American psychologist Irving Janis, in 1972. It refers to a decision-making tendency, when a small group of people with solid cohesion fail to express their individual goals, thoughts, passion, and values, and instead aim for the same direction.[10]

The sales department is no different. As in the case of Company X, if only leaders speak during the meetings and no one offers an opinion, there is a risk of making wrong decisions due to groupthink. Sales departments should aim for the establishment of collective intelligence, through free information-sharing and communication instead.

In 2020, one of the most innovative cases in the world was the COVID-19 drive-through testing. It was a groundbreaking method, which reduced the time required for the testing, as well as the additional infections that could occur during the testing process. This testing method, proposed by the doctor of the first confirmed COVID-19 patient in Korea, was introduced worldwide by adding additional ideas from several other doctors. In other words, a kind of collective intelligence worked. The advantage of collective intelligence is that in resolving a specific issue, opinions from experts in the field and diverse people can innovatively collaborate and solve the problem.

To make flexible use of collective intelligence, many organizations make great efforts to formalize the know-how and knowledge of their members from tacit knowledge. Knowledge Management is representative, which includes documenting cases of the in-house best practices, manualizing processes, and disseminating them. In particular, many companies introduce and adopt such systems or procedures to help maximize their performance, such as B2B sales, automobiles, insurance sales, and restaurant businesses, where processes are essential.

Turning Company X's sales information into data and then systematizing it to increase sales efficiency in the COVID-19 era is also a kind of Knowledge Management, where collective intelligence is in action. According to a study by Professor Raymond at The Ohio State University, knowledge-sharing significantly impacts organizational creativity, innovation, and performance improvement. However, corporate members hesitate to share their know-how, despite these positive effects. The unwillingness to share is even more profound for sales teams, such as Company X's sales department.[11] Organizational members tend to hesitate and hide when they are being compelled to disclose data and share knowledge for extrinsic motivational factors (compensation, appraisal, promotion); that is, if they feel controlled by managers and try to avoid punishment, they are more likely to hesitate and end up not sharing.[12]

Therefore, instead of compelling organizational members to follow the system, it is essential to let them recognize the value of knowledge management and encourage voluntary participation. As mentioned earlier, the director of Company X spent plenty of time explaining and communicating the benefits and importance of establishing the system. In particular, instead of letting the employees feel they were being managed or controlled, the director helped them realize that the organization could become healthier, and employees' competencies could be strengthened. And the team and each team member could also grow through this opportunity. During this process, the management and leadership support must continue.

A culture that only values results? No! A culture that takes process into account? Yes!

So far, we have looked at why the changes and communications are challenging, and the corresponding solutions. So, what is the most critical solution to make the information flow of sales departments transparent, and enable communication throughout the entire department? Top management and leaders' perceptions should be the starting point. No matter how magnificent the introduced system or procedures are, if the only focus is on performance and results, will the transparent information-sharing, communication, data, and knowledge necessary for sales be guaranteed and secured?

Probably not. For example, marketing costs were invested in sales exhibitions in regions you have not participated in, to secure new dealers in the Americas. Suppose your organizational culture is stingy with failures, and values only results. In that case, salespeople in charge of the corresponding regions would hesitate to participate in the exhibition, due to the fear of taking on the responsibilities of the investments, hiding the results, or even reporting false information. New activities, innovations, and attempts would become tardy and sluggish under such an organizational culture.

Carol Dweck, a professor at Stanford University known for her work on mindset, emphasizes, "Adequately praise for the efforts over the results." She also argues that organizations should aim for a learning-oriented culture (motivate their employees to learn) through which information and knowledge possessed by individuals can be disseminated throughout the entire organization.

People hastily stop taking risks if they feel that work performance or results are the only indicators of their abilities. However, if the organization deems it meaningful to learn in the process, through which the tacit and explicit knowledge can be brought back to the organization, new attempts and innovations will become more frequent. This is the same in departments where performance and figures are essential, such as sales and marketing teams. Eventually, the perspective on performance and process must change.

However, it takes quite a lot of time to change perspectives. As a result, you have to devote and invest time to bring about change, and make a difference. No matter how much this culture is emphasized and built, the team leader often leads the conversation at the beginning of the meeting. But at this time, silence should not be accepted. Team members should be encouraged to express their opinions, even a little; the discussion should never focus on criticizing or rebuking an employee. Many leaders make mistakes in this aspect. Of course, feedback should be given regarding errors and faults, but the focus of the meeting should never be punishment. In addition, to revitalize team communication, approaches considering the characteristics of the sales department should be utilized, such as message boards or business communication platforms like MS Teams. These communication tools were developed the most during COVID.

Importance of changing the perspective of performance & process

Type	Performance-oriented perspective	Performance and process-oriented perspective
Perceptions on appraisal	• All work should be evaluated based on the result.	• Employees should be honest about their performance, but it is meaningful to grow and learn throughout the process. (Growth is also included in the appraisal)
Goals	• Numbers need to be made. • Failure is unacceptable.	• Employees are allowed to fail. • 'How to make the process meaningful when thriving for better results' is critical..
Perspectives regarding outstanding talents	• Employees who deliver results regardless of the situation are highly valued, and sharing and disseminating information are unimportant.	• Employees with solid determinations for achieving results but value learning in the process, actively sharing their know-how, and reproducing knowledge are highly valued.

Outcome	• Members are obsessed with results; they fear failures and hide in the process instead of sharing.	• Fast learning and continuous improvement/development are achieved through active sharing of the process and honest discussions

Leaders who have to produce numbers and visible results are often thirsty for visualization of sales and marketing activities. This is even more so in the COVID-19 era, when there are fewer opportunities to meet offline. Therefore, many attempts are made to promote performance through changes in the sales information-sharing system and the way of working. However, it is not easy to succeed. Suppose leaders only focus on results, keep criticizing and reprimanding their employees, and adopt a vertical organizational structure and culture. In that case, successful changes in how they work, prevention of groupthink, and establishment of collective intelligence will be a long way off. As a result, successful changes can only be realized with the leaders' continuous interest and support, and the promotion of changes considering the specific organizational culture. Simultaneously, the periodical changes and collaboration of corporate members should also follow.

Now, it's time to strengthen the resilience of the sales department

As in the case introduced earlier, changes in the business environment of the sales departments, and in the way they work, are a tremendous burden on the team. Sometimes, although sales activities are reduced, some sales departments do not differ from before, and some sales teams have raised issues about the efficiency of human resources as they switch to online sales. These situations can cause stress and anxiety for salespeople. And even if many sales are shifted online, salespeople and their job are essential. It takes a long time for the final decision to be made during B2B sales, because it is necessary for salespeople to manage their customer relationships at each sales stage. In B2C sales, the role of salespeople in insurance, pharmaceutical, and medical equipment sales, where face-to-face sales are the leading channels, is still essential. Salespeople are still the focal point and point of contact when it comes to approaching customers. Though customer information may be received online, the salespeople are still very likely to be the ones to close a deal.

Efforts are essential to increase the department's resilience so that the sales team and its salespeople can adapt well to the changing environment, and continue producing results. And the success or failure of these efforts depends mainly on the leaders. In psychology, "psychological resilience" is the ability to mentally or emotionally know if one can cope with stress or hardships, effectively utilize internal and external resources, and convert these crises into experiences.[13]

In other words, resilience refers to the overall ability to adapt to the changing environment and use the experiences as advantageous to oneself. Though we have looked at the necessary competencies of salespeople and leaders in the COVID-19 era, in reality, the essential competency in the post-COVID age is 'resilience'.

Many people misunderstand when talking about resilience, thinking that optimistic people have high resilience. Of course, hopeful thinking is an essential factor. However, it can only be applied to situations where people can face reality without distorting it. Jim Collins, the author of Good to Great, said that he used to think resilience might be related to optimism. But this idea was changed after an interview with General Jim Stockdale, who was held captive in Vietnam for eight years.

When asked, "What kind of people did not survive the prisoner-of-war camp?" General Jim Stockdale said as follows:

"Oh, that's simple. The optimists. They said, 'they would release us at Christmas.' However, it was gradually pushed back from Christmas to Easter, Independence Day, Thanksgiving, and the Christmas of the following year. I think that they all died of disappointment."[14]

General Jim Stockdale, who survived eight years of prison life, had a cool-headed sense of reality that was crucial for his survival. At the same time, other prisoners who were very optimistic, were eventually discouraged by the gap with reality. We are not saying to think negatively, but to think positively while maintaining a sense of reality.

So, what efforts should be made to increase the organization's resilience? First, we have to face reality like General Stockdale. The priority will be to look closely at our situation, and the issues that must be resolved due to COVID-19. Next, we must create a culture where leaders trust and respect corporate members. During the pandemic, leaders communicating only with numbers and results, and managing only the progress of the work, does not help increase the organization's resilience. In the New Normal era, the attitudes and competencies necessary for leaders are not positive and result-oriented ways of thinking, but rather attitudes that encourage trying out new things and learning from the process.

According to Professor Kim Joo-hwan of Yonsei University, author of Resilience, people with low resilience tend to accept the changing environment or failures in an excessively negative way. Suppose leaders regard the work results negatively, or emphasize the negative over the positive in situations post-COVID. In that case, a culture of negativity will spread throughout the organization, which will eventually affect the organization's resilience. However, the sales departments are not the only ones experiencing difficulties. Everyone is having a hard time. Instead of being pessimistic, it is time to have confidence in overcoming challenges by valuing the positive aspects of change. Of course, as emphasized earlier, organizations should also face reality.

Ultimately, it's a matter of perspective

Among Western fairy tales, there is a story called "Percy the Pink." Percy was a big fan of pink color; he only owned pink items, including his clothes. Even the food he ate every day was pink. But Percy was not satisfied, since there were countless colors other than pink outside the castle he lived in. After consideration, Percy, the King of pink, enacted a law that made all his possessions and subjects pink. The people were forced to change everything to pink, because it was the king's order. But Percy was still not satisfied, since there were still many things out there that were not pink. So this time, all plants and animals in the country were dyed pink. Animals were even stained pink as soon as they were born. Finally, everything in the world seemed to have turned pink. But there was one thing that didn't change. It was the sky. No matter how omnipotent the king was, it was impossible to turn the sky pink. The king ordered his wise man to come up with a solution. The wise man, who had been struggling day and night, found a trick, which was glasses. The wise man told the king to put on the glasses he had prepared for him and look up at the sky, and the sky would be changed to pink. Percy was pleased and satisfied to see that the sky had turned pink.[15]

It is a silly fairy tale, but if you think about it, it is very profound. We live in the world we think of. The results can vary significantly depending on what glasses we use, or what perspective we use to look at the world.

Throughout this book, we discussed the change of perspectives in the post-COVID-19 era, and the leaders' thoughts and views. Pivoting in the business is a shift in perspective, and various ways to tackle organizational problems are also perspectives. Theory X versus Theory Y, open learning versus enclosed learning, groupthink versus collective intelligence, fixed mindsets versus growth mindsets, and result-oriented thinking versus process-oriented thinking all depend on how leaders view and lead the organization.

Change is always tricky and uncomfortable. In particular, changing the existing familiar way of working is accompanied by plenty of pain. The change cannot be easily adapted by many sales departments and salespeople, who suddenly have to change their offline and network-oriented sales practices. However, in the post-COVID-19 era, online meetings and product demonstrations through webinars will increase, and online non-face-to-face operations will become increasingly natural. Ultimately, who can adapt to new rules first, and create competitiveness within change, will be an essential measure of the success or failure of a company in the future. In that sense, COVID-19 is presenting new challenges to existing sales departments and teams.

EPILOGUE

Two years have already passed since the outbreak of COVID-19. It was awkward wearing a mask before, but now people cannot live without it. In addition, offline education, events, and meetings are naturally being conducted online, and people have become familiar with such an environment. It is said that humans adapt to changes, but now that adapting has become so natural, it is even a little scary. Fortunately, with the popularization of vaccines, people have started to expect COVID-19 to end soon. However, there are many rumors regarding the end of COVID-19. Some say that COVID-19 will quickly end if herd immunity is realized, and our life will naturally return to its previous routine, while others say that life will never be able to go back to how it was before.

What do you think?

We definitely do not think we will be able to return to the same world as before COVID-19. The question we need to consider should not be "when will we be able to go back to before COVID-19" but "how to adapt and change in the New Normal era." Honestly speaking, at the beginning of COVID-19, we also thought it wouldn't last long.。 (At that time, we were consulting for overseas agencies and corporations in Latin America, Africa, and Eurasia.) However, these expectations were shattered. Fortunately(?) we quickly adapted to the change. The work that used to be conducted through business trips was shifted to online meetings and conferences, and offline education also adapted to the COVID-19 era by making many changes to both the content and the delivery method. Because of COVID-19, we had concerns and picked up various know-how in resolving issues and problems faced by many customers. Simultaneously we started writing those down, thinking, "Why don't we share these with others?"

As seen in this book, companies that pursued rapid change and aggressive innovation in response to COVID-19, such as remote work, online purchase and service support for customers, the introduction of advanced operating technologies, supply chain adjustment, and switching to the cloud, created many success stories, including 3 times the growth, 2.5 times the financial outcomes, and 4.8 times the innovation achievements compared to those that did not embrace change.[1]

What changes are you experiencing, and how are you responding to those changes? Do you still have the hope that everything will go back to how it was before? Unfortunately, even if our daily lives return to the previous normal, our way of working will not be 100% the same. In particular, sales departments and teams will experience more changes and challenges.

Many sales activities shifted from offline to online by utilizing various video conferencing tools, such as Zoom and Teams. Even large-scale exhibitions and conferences were converted to live conferences, or held through online platforms. As a result, the concerns of sales teams and business leaders who carried out various sales activities last year are starting now. Since we have already realized that we can conduct some of our sales activities online, we need to consider whether online or offline sales activities are more suitable in the future. And if online activities are considered better, then it will be necessary to consider what kind of content should be delivered, and which communication method should be used to approach customers. In other words, instead of sticking to a confident approach regarding a specific sales activity or a particular issue, we should flexibly utilize online, offline, or even hybrid methods, depending on the situation and occasion. In addition, as discussed throughout this book, leaders also need to change and develop their relevant competencies in various areas, such as the sales departments' way of working, the organizations' operations, performance management, coaching and feedback, and change management.

No one knows how the world will change in the future. Instead, uncertainty may accelerate, and the pace of change may be faster. And the future can be more unstable and worrying because of this uncertainty. However, uncertainty is not necessarily a bad thing.

Innovation has a strong correlation to change and uncertainty. Uncertainty makes us continue to innovate and develop. This is because confronting uncertainty is an innovative way to respond to change.

This book discusses the perspectives and worldviews we should be equipped with at the changing point. It's actually up to us to decide whether to be changed, or to lead the change. Many people start to exercise after a medical checkup. This is because many office employees, including ourselves, are advised by doctors to diet and exercise. But what's interesting is that it's hard and painful to go on a diet after being recommended to go on one. We even start craving soju, pork belly, chicken, and beer, which we usually don't crave. However, if I decide to build up my body through weight training, I exercise more passionately than when someone else tells me to. This is the difference between "someone compels you and suggests you do it" and "you take the initiative and lead." The same applies to change. As in the latter case, you can become a change leader and devote more passion.

The burden of accepting and adapting to the changes falls on us. In the era of New Normal in sales, the journey to change will never be easy. And it won't be easy to succeed by simply imitating what others do. It is time to deeply consider the suitable method for us, and how we should develop and carry it forward. In this era of New Normal, we hope you can become the ones to take the initiative in leading the change, and create your successful experiences and stories instead of being forced to follow.

REFERENCES

Prologue

1. http://www.asiae.co.kr/news/viewhtm?idxno=2017051910292542264
2. 이장주, 진정성 있는 세계관으로 메타버스 세대 공략, DBR 2021 3월 Issue 2
3. https://www.sciencetimes.co.kr/news/코로나19로_인해_일상이_바뀌다/
4. https://www.the-stock.kr/news/articleView.html?idxno=13479

Chapter 1

1. 로날트 D. 게르슈테, 강희진 옮김, 『질병이 바꾼 세계의 역사』, 미래의 창(2020), 33.
2. 남대일, 전략적 변곡점, LG경제연구소(2003)
3. 한국농수산식품유통공사(aT)의 가공식품 세분시장 현황 보고서(2020)
4. 한국일보, 코로나19 시대의 생존전략, '피버팅하라'
   https://www.hankookilbo.com/News/Read/A2020112713140002142
5. 내셔널지오그래픽, 브레인게임5,
   https://www.youtube.com/watch?v=OsiSBYCC53E
6. Pashler(1988), Familiarity and visual change detection, Perception & Psychophysics, 44 (4), 369-378.
7. MacKay(2003). Inattentional blindness: Looking without seeing, Current Directions in Psychological Science, 180-184.
8. 기획재정부(2020), https://biz.chosun.com/site/data/html_dir/2020/12/01/2020120102552.html
9. https://ko.tradingeconomics.com/
10. https://www.beveragedaily.com/Article/2020/05/04/PepsiCo-Tailoring-innovation-around-coronavirus
11. https://www.audi.de/de/brand/de/live-demo.html

Chapter 2

1. 장효상, 민승기, 짧은 시간에 더 명확하게 정보전달, 영업 직원의 디지털 무장 더 중요해져(DBR 2020 6월 issue 2)
2. McKinsey&Company, The B2B digital inflection point: How sales have changed during COVID-19, April 30, 2020
3. https://www.business2community.com/infographics/b2b-sales-impact-of-coronavirus-infographic-02304040
4. Jason Jordan, Robert Kelly, Companies with a Formal Sales Process Generate More Revenue, HBR January 21, 2015
5. Jason Jordan, Robert Kelly, Companies with a Formal Sales Process Generate More Revenue, HBR January 21, 2015
6. https://www.mk.co.kr/news/it/view/2020/08/849956/

Chapter 3

1. 장효상, 민승기, 자율성과 권한위임으로 성과지표를 '피버팅'하라. DBR 2020 11월 issue 2
2. Campbell, Donald T (1979). "Assessing the impact of planned social change". Evaluation and Program Planning. 2 (1): 67–90.
3. Peter Cappelli and Anna Tavis, The Performance Management Revolution, HBR October 2016
4. https://www.forbes.com/sites/davidburkus/2016/06/01/how-adobe-scrapped-its-performance-review-system-and-why-it-worked/#3299dd0955e8
5. Douglas McGregor's Theory X and Theory Y (1960, MIT Sloan School of Management)
6. 폴잭, 이주영 역, 『트러스트 팩터』, 매일경제신문사(2018), 78.

7. Mary S. Logan and Daniel C. Ganster, "The Effects of Empowerment on Attitudes and Performance: The Role of Social Support and Empowerment Beliefs," Journal of Management Studies 44, no. 8 (2007): 1523-1550.
8. Linda A. Hill, Greg Brandeau, Emily Truelove, and Kent Lineback, Collective Genius: The Art and Practice of Leading Innovation (Cambridge: Harvard Business Review Press, 2014)
9. Deci, Edward. (1971). The Effects of Externally Mediated Rewards on Intrinsic Motivation. Journal of Personality and Social Psychology. 18. 105-115.
10. Deci, Edward L.; Ryan, Richard M. (1985). Intrinsic Motivation and Self-Determination in Human Behavior
11. http://performance-appraisals.org/faq/rankyank.htm
12. 대니얼 카니먼 지음, 이창신 옮김, 『생각에 관한 생각』, 김영사(2018), 621.
13. https://www.vuca-world.org
14. 더글라스 무크 지음, 진성록 옮김, 『당신의 고정관념을 깨뜨릴 심리실험 45가지』, 부글북스(2007), 156-157.

Chapter 4

1. http://news.kmib.co.kr/article/view.asp?arcid=0924157411&code=11151400 국민일보, 2020-09-26, 나도 모르는 내 취향까지 읽는다… 초개인화, 끝 어딘가
2. 캐럴 드웩 지음, 김준수 옮김, 『마인드셋』, 스몰빅라이프(2017)
3. If Pandemic Productivity Is Up, Why Is Innovation Slowing Down?, Knowledge @ Wharton, Prof. Michael Parke, Nov 10, 2020
4. Amy C. Edmondson, Gene Daley, How to Foster Psychological Safety in Virtual Meetings, HBR, August 25, 2020
5. 롤프 도벨리 지음, 두행숙 옮김, 『스마트한 생각들』, 걷는 나무(2012), 58-60.

6. Bar-Eli, M., Azar, O. H., Ritov, I., Keidar-Levin, Y., & Schein, G. (2007). Action bias among elite soccer goalkeepers: The case of penalty kicks. Journal of Economic Psychology, 28(5), 606-621.
7. Tom DeMarco, 류한석/이별철/황재선 옮김, 『슬랙(Slack)』, 인사이트(2010)
8. McChrystal, Team of Teams: New Rules of Engagement for a complex World, 216~217.
9. 마커스 버킹엄, 애슐리 구달 지음, 이영래 옮김, 『일에 관한 9가지 거짓말』, 쌤앤 파커스(2019)

Chapter 5

1. 질리언 테트 지음, 신예경 옮김, 『사일로 이펙트, 무엇이 우리를 눈 멀게 하는가』, 어크로스(2016), 92-97.
2. 김현기, 전략을 실패로 이끄는 5가지 함정, LG 경제연구원, 2014. 9. 15
3. Roger L. Martin, The Execution Trap, Harvard Business Review, 2010 July-August
4. Donald N. Sull, Closing the gap between strategy and execution, MIT Sloan Management Review, 2007
5. Gary L. Neilson, Karla L. Martin, and Elizabeth Powers, The Secrets to Successful Strategy Execution, Harvard Business Review, 2008 June
6. 김민주, 『시장의 흐름이 보이는 경제 법칙 101』, 위즈덤 하우스(2011)
7. 장재웅, 상효이재, 『네이키드 애자일』, 미래의 창(2019), 176~183.
8. Kevan Hall, Making the Matrix Work: How Matrix Managers Engage People and Cut Through Complexity, Hodder & Stoughton, 2013
9. "Manifesto for Agile Software Development", Agile Manifesto, accessed September 10, 2017, http://Agilemanifesto.org/
10. Thoren. Pia-Maria, 『Agile People』, Lioncrest Publishing, 42 page
11. https://www.hankyung.com/economy/article/202101309444i
12. 임홍택, 『90년대생이 온다』, 웨일북(2018), 115.

Chapter 6

1. 원지현, 조직의 변화, 구성원의 구체적 행동 변화에서부터, LG경제연구원, 2014-11-09.
2. Brehm, J. W. (1966). A theory of psychological reactance. Academic Press
3. jonahberger.com/videos, 조나 버거 지음, 김원호 옮김, 『캐털리스트』, 문학동네(2020)
4. Colin M. Fisher, Teresa M. Amabile, and Julianna Pillemer, How to Help (Without Micromanaging), HBR January–February 2021
5. https://ioadvisory.com/being-ourselves-vs-covering-at-work/
6. 우리는 왜 대학에 가는가 5부, EBS, 2014, https://www.youtube.com/watch?v= fem5SG5YjaY
7. 에이미 에드먼슨, 최윤영 옮김, 『두려움 없는 조직』, 다산북스(2019)
8. https://culturepulsconsulting.com/2018/03/10/how-to-develop-psychological-safety/
9. https://www.nytimes.com/2020/03/23/world/asia/coronavirus-south-korea-flatten-curve.html
10. Paul't Hart. "Irving L. Janis' Victims of Groupthink." Political Psychology, vol. 12, no. 2, 1991, 247–278.
11. Wang, S., & Noe, R. A. (2010). Knowledge sharing: A review and directions for future research. Human Resource Management Review, 20(2), 115–131.
12. Marylène Gagné, Amy Wei Tian, Christine Soo, Bo Zhang, Khee Seng Benjamin Ho and Katrina Hosszu, Why Employees Don't Share Knowledge with Each Other, HBR July 19, 2019
13. 김주환, 『회복탄력성』, 위즈덤하우스(2019)
14. 다이앤 L. 쿠투 외 지음, 김수미 옮김, 『회복탄력성』, 21세기북스(2017), 15~16.
15. 최인철, 『프레임, 나를 바꾸는 심리학의 지혜』, 21세기북스(2021), 25.

EPILOGUE

1. https://www.mk.co.kr/opinion/contributors/view/2020/10/1113270/

www.ingramcontent.com/pod-product-compliance
Lightning Source LLC
Chambersburg PA
CBHW072001110526
44592CB00012B/1170